Sweet Freedom Whispered in My Ear

by Shirley Buck

RHG | MEDIA PRODUCTIONS™

Sweet Freedom Whispered in My Ear

Copyright © 2022 by Shirley Buck

RHG Media Productions
25495 Southwick Drive #103
Hayward, CA 94544.

ISBN 979-8-9891215-0-2 (paperback)
ISBN 979-8-9891215-1-9 (hardcover)

Visit us on line at www.YourPurposeDrivenPractice.com
Printed in the United States of America.

WHAT PEOPLE ARE SAYING

"*Sweet Freedom Whispered in My Ear* feels like a beacon of light shining through the darkness."
—*Tiffani Freckleton, RN, nurse coach, author of* My NICU Story: Written With Love *and co-author of the award-winning international bestseller* Letters to a Future Nurse

"Shirley's journey from a turbulent beginning to a place of peace, success and contentment is a testament to her courage."
—*Suzanne Mealer*

"The author's deep understanding of trauma and abuse recovery shines through every page, offering practical guidance and real-life situations that readers can relate to."
—*Courtney Fassett*

"This book has captivated my soul."
—*Marie Jones, LMT*

"*Sweet Freedom Whispered in My Ear* is a riveting true story of the power of the human spirit's ability to overcome even the most unfathomable traumas."
—*Lisa Molidor, RN*

CONTENTS

ACKNOWLEDGMENTS

I would like to thank my children Ryan and Aubrey first and foremost —not only for believing in me and supporting my decision to write a book, but for being the main reason for me to continue to succeed in my adult life and not give up. You both are the core of my soul, my love and joy. I will always do anything for you both.

I'd also like to thank my grandchildren Landon and Leilah. They were my laughter throughout writing this book. It can take a bit of an emotional toll on anyone revisiting experiences like these, even with the tools I possess to change my thought patterns to change my emotions. Through my grandchildren I was able to maintain magic, laughter and happiness throughout the creation of this book. Landon and Leilah, I love you both more than you can imagine.

Nickole, you have been an incredible source of motivation since you were born. I am at a loss of words when I try to express how much you mean to me. When I see you smile... 123...

My best friend Suzanne Mealer, Together we have traveled the vast majority of the contents of this book. Despite the few hiatuses in our friendship,we have maintained our bond which I believe can never be broken. I cannot describe the significance you hold within my life.Thank you for your unwavering belief in me.

My biggest fan, Steve Wegrzyn: I don't know how many times I cried on your shoulder from pure exhaustion or self doubt. You always believed in me and my abilities.

To Rebecca Hall Gruyter, my publisher, thank you for your support and exceptional guidance throughout the publishing journey of my book. Your dedication to bring my vision to life has been truly remarkable. I am deeply grateful for being able to feel comfortable and safe speaking with you.

Last, but not least, to Beth Myers: You rekindled a fire that this time was not extinguished.

For all of you I am extremely grateful.

There are many people who have been very supportive and helpful. Please forgive me if I did not mention every one. Please know you are greatly appreciated.

I hope I met and exceeded your expectations and am worthy of your love and support.

PROLOGUE

February 2nd, 1981

I spent the weekend with my father in his trailer in Hegewisch, a small community on the south side of Chicago. My parents were divorced, so traveling between homes wasn't unusual. After a rather dull visit, I was looking forward to being back home —but not so much to seeing my mother, although things did seem to be getting better between us.

I arrived home to my mother's apartment on the north side of Chicago. I had to ring the doorbell several times. When rung, the doorbell would set off a series of lights flashing in our apartment. Both my parents were deaf, so that was the method they each had to let them know someone was at the door. I began to think my mother wasn't home, which wasn't unusual for her. I would just have to retrieve the spare keys from our neighbors who lived in the basement of our apartment building.

I heard the door to our apartment open. My mother looked down the stairs to where I was waiting to be let in. She signed with her hands, and, with the best voice she could muster up (I was one of the few people who could understand her speech), she said, "Shirley is not home. "

I was truly confused. How could she not recognize me? I signed back to her: *I am Shirley, your daughter.* She shrugged her shoulders and buzzed me in.

I noticed she had lost weight just within the weekend that I was gone, and she smelled as if she hadn't bathed for a couple of days. I asked her if she was okay, and once again she shrugged her shoulders. I was trying to figure out what was going on, and then the lights that signal someone was at the door began flashing. It was our landlord. I was truly concerned about him seeing her so disheveled and confused. He had come over to collect the rent and to explain that our rent soon would be lowered, but we would be paying our own gas bill. I signed to my mother, interpreting what the landlord was saying. She started screaming and yelling that he was trying to trick us into something and trying to take advantage of us, so I had to politely apologize for my mother's behavior and ask the landlord to leave. I told him I would explain things to her at a better time and everything would be okay.

I wanted to make sure she ate something. She certainly seemed as though she needed to. So I went to go look for something to make for her. It wasn't unusual not to have food in the house. That was always a challenge as she usually sold our food stamps to purchase alcohol. I noticed there wasn't even any beer in the house. Now, that was unusual.

All I could find was packages of Jell-O and pudding mix. Remarkably, we had milk, so I made her both. She ate very little of it, but I thought it was good that she ate something.

I felt as if the day was going in slow motion. She barely talked to me at all. She pulled up a chair by the window in our very small kitchen and stared out of it most of the day.

When it was time to go to bed, she asked if I would please sleep with her. I was so uneasy with her behavior that day that I grabbed a crucifix that my grandmother had given me and put it under my pillow—for some sort of comfort, I guess. Throughout that day, I was so excitedly waiting for school. I didn't mind school, but I don't ever remember being so excited and wanting to go so desperately as I did that day.

I believe that keeping positive thoughts and imagining myself going to school were crucial to my survival that night. When I look back, I can still feel how strong that feeling was. I went through most of my life being afraid of being excited about something because I didn't want to jinx it. This is yet another experience in my life that leads to me knowing now that keeping positive thoughts and keeping your vibration high is so important in any situation. Learning these kinds of lessons led, in my later years, to my knowledge of training my mind to change my life.

I woke at 2:00 a.m. and noticed my mother was not in bed. I started to head out of the bedroom to go find her, but I stopped and turned around to grab my crucifix to bring with me. I decided against it. I proceeded to go look for her and found her in the kitchen sitting in the same chair she had been sitting in most of that day. I slowly approached her. I felt my stomach tighten with fear as I tapped her on the shoulder and asked if she was okay.

She stood up and hugged me. She hugged me so tight that it made me feel claustrophobic and scared. I tried to back away, and she grabbed me by the hair and started punching me. The blows were very painful, worse than any of the other times she had hit me.

She then bashed my head into a fish tank, stuck her fingers down my throat, and started pulling up on whatever she could grab in my throat. The fear I was feeling now was sheer terror. I thought I was probably going to die.

I bit down on her hand as hard as I could, and she pulled her hand out and went to go get a knife. In the meantime, the lights in the apartment started flashing again. I felt a quick glimpse of hope. My neighbors were trying to get into the house due to all the screaming and noise they were hearing.

I looked at my mother, and I looked at the door. She started coming at me with a knife. I ran for the door. As I reached the door and was frantically trying to open it, I noticed she wasn't behind me. I don't know why, but I looked back down the hallway at her.

She looked at me and violently started to stab herself repeatedly in the stomach and throat. I was so shocked that I didn't know what to do. Somehow, I managed to run down the stairs to the neighbors who lived in the basement apartment. They helped me inside and called the police. I remember waiting for what seemed like an eternity for them to arrive. They finally did. I explained to them what I had seen.

They asked, " She's deaf?"

I said yes.

The police responded by saying that if they were going to enter the apartment, I would have to go with them.

I was absolutely terrified, and I refused.

My neighbors said, " Look at her! Does she seem like she is in any condition to enter that apartment?" My face was bruised and badly swollen. My nightgown was tattered and torn.

My mother had almost taken my life, and I wasn't about to go back in there again. What happened next was beyond our belief.

The police officers left. They told us to call a relative to come help us with the situation.

In the meantime, we had called my father's neighbor. I had his number in case there was an emergency and I had to get hold of my father, who, as I have mentioned, was also deaf. The neighbor went and woke my father and told him there was an emergency at my house. My father showed up, and we called the police once again and they went up with him. After a short while, my father came into the bedroom where the neighbors had me resting. He looked at me with an expression I'd never seen on his face before. He signed to me, *Your mother is dead.* I know if it had not been for those neighbors ringing our doorbells, she would have taken my life as well.

I spent the next few hours answering the same questions over and over again from different police officers. By the time they were done questioning me, it was daylight. After determining that I was miraculously okay physically, they removed my mother's body. My father drove me to his trailer. I told myself, *She probably isn't dead. They probably took her to an institution and didn't want to reveal that to me.* The mind is a fascinating coping mechanism.

My father told me to try and get some sleep. I'm not sure I slept much. I do know I woke with a splitting headache, an aching body, and a desperate need to find out this was just a nightmare. When I stepped outside and saw my father look at me, I knew it wasn't. It was as real as real can be.

My father explained that we had some things to take care of that day. First on our list was going back to my mother's apartment. My stomach was in knots. I couldn't bear to go back there, but he said we didn't have a choice. He made us some breakfast, and I watched in disbelief as he ate. I could barely force a couple of morsels of food into my mouth, and I couldn't believe he could eat. He explained in detail how he'd found my mother the night before. He handed me a partial denture she'd had in her mouth. He said it must have flown out of her mouth while she was stabbing herself. It was covered in bloody specks. He didn't explain this to me out of cruelty —some deaf parents, especially in that era, lacked a knowledge of how to filter things.

The entire drive back to her place, I felt as though I was going to throw up. I didn't know how I was going to get through the day. I started to daydream about the future. I distracted myself with thoughts of a new life.

When we arrived, the feeling of anguish returned. We walked in, and I looked around in disbelief. There was a huge puddle of blood on the kitchen floor. I felt as though I was in a dream —or, rather, a nightmare. I looked around some more. There were handprints of blood all over the walls and the doorway moulding. I imagined my mother staggering around all alone and wondered if she was afraid. I had always been her protector. I felt so devastated and guilty.

My father returned from his truck with buckets and mops. He handed me one of each, and we started to clean up my dead mother's blood. I couldn't even cry. The feeling I felt is not one I can describe even to this day. When we were finished cleaning the floors and walls, I went to retrieve my pets. My hamster was in his cage, dead. I couldn't believe it. What kind of cruel joke was the world playing on me? I searched for my cat. I found her under my bed; naturally she was hiding in fear. I decided to feed her before we left. Even the can of cat food had blood on it.

Before we left, I went into my mother's room to get the crucifix I had placed under my pillow. Intuition must have prompted me, and I looked under her pillow as well. She also had a crucifix on a necklace placed under her pillow. I guess I wasn't the only one afraid that night. Later, I gave that necklace to her best friend.

I don't remember how we were informed, but the next step was identifying my mother's body at the morgue. When we arrived, my father entered with me in tow. I did all of the interpreting, as usual. They led us both into a room with a projection screen, on which they showed us a close-up of a face. It was my mother. I felt a sharp pain in my stomach and a tightness in my chest. I wanted to cry or scream out in anger, but I couldn't do either. I then felt a numbness come over me, and that feeling stayed with me for years whenever I thought about my mother's suicide.

She had a big scratch on her forehead. I couldn't help but think I had caused that scratch during the fight for my life. Crazy, I know, compared to what she had done to herself, but I was carrying a lot of guilt, and that was one other thing to add to the list. I coincidentally had a very similar scratch on my forehead as well. Of course that was very minimal compared to the other bruising and swelling on my face, but I thought it strange that my scratch was so similar to hers.

She didn't have a regular wake or funeral. My father came up with $800 for at least some kind of proper burial. It was all he could afford. My grandmother said it was better than potter's field.

The day arrived for her funeral. My face had to be covered in makeup to be presentable. On the way there, I remember thinking about the past few days and feeling a great desire for everything to finally be over. I was thirteen years old, yet I was alongside my father handling everything that had to be done. After all, I was his ears and voice. I was used to handling my parents' responsibilities, but this situation was above and beyond what a child should have to endure.

Only a handful of people came to the funeral. The closed casket was wheeled in, and it looked as though it was a cardboard box covered in gray felt. I'd attended a few wakes and funerals already, and this casket was nothing like the ones I had seen before. I felt sad for my mother. At the end of her life, all she had was a few people present, an impersonal sermon read, and a very basic box to be laid to rest in. Although I felt pain, I also felt gratitude that, thanks to my father, she at least had that much. It definitely could have been even less.

Weeks went by, and I had to settle in at a new school. I was just going through the motions. That numbness was at the core of my soul. I didn't know if I was ever going to feel anything again.

My father informed me that I had received $1,000 from some insurance policy my mother had. He asked me what I wanted to do with it. I told him I wanted to buy my mother a headstone for her grave, and that he could have the rest of the money to pay him back what I could for her funeral.

I'm so grateful that I did so. We purchased a headstone for her. Even though I haven't been to her grave very often, I feel better knowing she at least had someone care enough about her to have some kind of marker.

I didn't cry about this situation until I was about twenty-nine years old.

This was not the beginning of my abuse, nor nearly the end of it. Within these pages, you will encounter tales of abuse and trauma, stories that may stir your emotions and awaken your empathy. But I implore you, dear reader, to venture forth and explore the entirety of this book. For within these chapters lies not only the darkness of the past but also the light of a beautiful outcome. This book is a testament to the resilience of the human spirit, offering invaluable tools and insights that can assist in overcoming the suffocating grip of anxiety and depression. Come, join me on this transformative voyage, and together let us discover the strength and healing that await us.

CHAPTER 1

BORN TO A WORLD OF SILENCE

I was born to deaf parents who were optimistic that my arrival might save their marriage. They had many marital problems to overcome. My mother never hesitated to tell me that they'd had me to save their marriage and that I had only made it worse.

When my mother was a child, she was both loved and very sheltered. I was told that her mother would hide her in a bedroom whenever visitors came over, as she was ashamed of her being deaf. She therefore grew up very insecure, which affected her marriage and life immensely. My father grew up going to a deaf school in Jacksonville, Illinois. He learned how to be confident and compete in sports and was always surrounded by a strong deaf community. He was also very lively and outgoing.

My dad and I were always close, although he was not the ideal father. When he was not in a relationship with someone, he would pick me up on weekends and take me on many outings. Wrestling matches and Cousin's restaurant in Hegewisch were some of my favorite outings. He took me to work with him some days when he had to.

He took me to church every Sunday that I was with him. I became an alternate service interpreter at the Stony Island Church of Christ.

SWEET FREEDOM WHISPERED IN MY EAR

He rode a Harley when I was young until an accident that broke thirty-three bones in his body robbed him of his passion for riding. I loved riding with him and feeling the wind blow through my hair. He was so proud that I wasn't afraid of riding. I remember wanting to be fearless like he was, not afraid of everything like Mom was.

After my dad's accident, my mother refused to take me to see him. When he came out of his coma, the only person he was asking for was me. He could not understand what had happened to him, and I was the only one who could rectify that. My paternal grandmother insisted someone go pick me up and bring me to the hospital immediately. She was his only other advocate.

So the police showed up and brought me to the hospital. I was seven years old, and there I was helping with yet another situation. Walking down the halls of the dimly lit hospital gave me a strong feeling of angst as I wondered what I would be facing. The smell alone was enough to make me nauseous.

When I arrived at his room in the ICU, I had to wait for some reason. There were nurses performing some procedure. I remember a nurse asking me if I wanted a coloring book and crayons while I was waiting to see him. Even though I was only seven years old, I thought she was crazy. I was there to find out what happened to my father and to be his voice, not to color or play with toys.

Looking back now, I realize how mature I was, being such a little girl yet having the ability to go into such a strange setting to help my deaf parent. He was so helpless and frail. They had him in traction for nine months. I visited him often and interpreted for the doctors and nurses about his condition.

As he began to heal, we spent many hours laughing and joking. He had a wonderful sense of humor and zest for life, even while in traction in a hospital.

He never laid a hand on me except slapping me across the face during a very emotional incident when I was fifteen years old, but that is a story I will tell you about later on. Unfortunately, whenever he was in a relationship, I would be placed upon a shelf until the relationship eventually ended. I suppose he was lonely and wanted companionship and I got in the way of that.

I absolutely loved my dad, and I know he loved me. He just had to find his own happiness no matter what the cost was —even at my expense.

He died suddenly without warning when I was thirty-three. I was devastated. I felt I finally had a real connection with my father, and he was taken from me way too soon. I got the call on October fourteenth. They didn't find him the day he died. He lived alone, so no one really missed him until he missed church. He attended without fail, so it caused suspicion, which led to a wellness check.

They said he had passed on the ninth. The ninth of October is my birthday. He called me on my birthday that year through a service that provided a relay between deaf and hearing people for phone conversations. He didn't usually remember my birthday, so it meant a lot to me. I was at my daughter's soccer game and I had forgotten my cell phone. I had a deep nagging feeling in my gut to leave the game, go home and get it. I didn't want to leave her game, but I felt I really had to. I knew I'd be back before the game was over. I walked in, and the phone was ringing with his call. Had I not left the game, I would have never received that call.

He died that night. This incident is one of the reasons I believe in following your gut instincts. These prompts and feelings are important and provide important connections and opportunities. Listen to them and follow them. Don't miss out. I believe my father listened to an instinct that prompted him to reach out to me, and I know I did in walking home for my phone. We had that opportunity for that last call.

He lived alone in Whitehall, Illinois. It was about a five-hour-plus drive for me. I hadn't wanted him to move so far away from me, but he wanted to live in a community with a large population of deaf people. My ex-husband and I helped him with the down payment for a large piece of land he had a trailer placed on.

Upon learning he had died, I headed out for the long drive to Whitehall. When I arrived, I felt that feeling of angst I had felt once before as I entered my mother's apartment after her death.

When I walked in, there was a very strong foul smell. It almost knocked me to my knees. I slowly walked into his room through a swarm of flies that seemed to battle my every step.

There was a puddle of blood on his bed. I proceeded into his bathroom, and bowel excretion covered the floor and left a trail leading to his bed. It felt as though my heart had stopped for a moment. I started to vomit from the combination of the smell and what I was seeing. I had to search for a bucket. I found two: one to clean with and one to vomit into while cleaning. This was a hard task, but especially hard when I was in still in shock over his death.

Once again, I was cleaning up the blood and mess from a deceased parent.

The loss of my father hit me extremely hard. We had finally became close again and stayed close after his third divorce. Starting when I was eighteen, I already had my own apartment, so I no longer longed for his guidance or support. We could finally be friends. I am very thankful for that. I am especially thankful for being a person who was able to forgive my father. Forgiveness is the true lesson here. Had I not chosen to forgive him, I would have missed some wonderful times with my father. From this time on, he stayed in my life and was even a part of his grandchildren's lives. He was an amazing guy full of life, and I miss him dearly.

Through this experience and many more, I have learned to follow my intuition. We are all equipped with intuition that, if followed through on, can save us from many hurtful and harmful situations. It takes a bit of practice, but quieting our minds from time to time enhances our awareness even when we arenot in that quiet state.

CHAPTER 2

A SILENT HOUSEHOLD

I grew up with the major responsibility of learning sign language pressed upon me. My parents had not stressed the importance of signing with my older brother, so the responsibility fell to me. My father was very adamant about me learning it. He would not speak to me unless I signed to him. I am grateful for that, as it is a blessing to know sign language. From a very young age, I also had to speak for my parents. I was told by my grandmother that I was not quite four when my mother had a fainting spell, and I was able to climb up on a chair and call my dad's place of employment to have him come home.

Our home was always filled with fighting. My mother was always starting fights with my father due to her insecurities. He couldn't even be five minutes late coming home from work without her having some sort of suspicion. When I was five years old, the dissolution of their marriage began. With my mother acting out one of her screaming fits and flushing yet another set of wedding rings down our toilet, my father finally left. Standing in front of the house, my father urging me to come with him and my mother begging me to stay, I was torn. I longed to go with my father, but I stayed with my mother because, even at that very early age, I knew she could not be left alone.

The next time I saw my dad was a few weeks later at a lawyer's office. I was there to help interpret the details of their divorce. My grandfather was also there, but he didn't know sign language, so the responsibility fell on me.

Life after that was pretty much filled with going back and forth between my dad's trailer in Hegewisch and my mother's home in Indiana. My mother got the house, and my grandfather paid most of her bills. There was always some kind of drama going on.

When I was almost eight, my mother met my stepfather. He drank a lot, prompting my mother to start drinking. Once she started, it didn't take long before she became a full-blown alcoholic. When she was drinking, all the anger and frustration would pour out of her, and she would take it out on me. It only progressed over the years. She'd had a serious case of depression for as long as I could remember. Unfortunately depression was not taken as seriously back then as it is today. To make matters worse, she was deaf and wasn't aware of the proper channels to go through to get help. Only when I became an adult did I begin to understand how helpless she truly was.

* * *

My stepfather would molest me from time to time. His explanation of it was that he was showing me love. I was very confused and talked to my dad about it. My father was still recovering from his accident at the time and was using a walker to get around, but he threatened my stepfather, and make no mistake, he got his point across. My father had him shaking with fear.

He never touched me again, but I felt sick being around him. Feeling his eyes on me and knowing what he was thinking about was devastating to me. The smell of beer always brought me back to the nights that he would take advantage of me anytime we were alone.

He would also abuse my mother. I witnessed a slap to the face here and there, but there was more severe abuse also; I saw the bruises and the way she cowered with fear around him. He tried to keep the worst of it from me, probably because he feared my father. When I questioned my mother about it, she would tell me to mind my own business and say things along the lines of *Don't you go telling your father or anyone else about it. This is my business.*

Eventually my mother's husband talked her into selling our home, after which we moved into a small, dirty apartment on the north side of Chicago. The comforts of my home were gone, and a musty smell seemed to follow me everywhere I walked in that place. I was so afraid there many nights, but especially my first night there. I woke in the night to get a glass of water and turned on the lights to witness a scattering of what seemed to be a hundred roaches fleeing. It's amazing what you can adapt to. Roaches and lack of food eventually became the norm to me.

My mother's husband then took all the money from the sale of our home and left us. He divorced my mother shortly after that, but not before spending the money he stole.

This of course led my mother to drink more. Frustration and anger consumed her, along with the alcohol. I was the only one there to be the recipient of the hurt she was trying so desperately to release.

I spent many nights with my grandfather and grandmother in their flat. I wasn't close to my grandmother. She was always angry that her husband would spoil their child (my mother), Margie. I was especially close to my grandfather. I'm not sure he knew about the abuse I was going through at the hands of my mother. If he did, I know he loved both of us and tried to protect us as much as possible. I once mentioned having been touched inappropriately, and he said, "We don't talk about those kinds of things." I guess it was just the times I was growing up in.

I loved going to my grandfather's home. He allowed me to sit on the front porch with him and the neighbors who would come over to join us. They would drink their beer and chat and I would feel so loved and safe. He took me on long walks through the neighborhood of Bucktown in Chicago. We would always stop at the candy store and he would let me pick out whatever I liked. He taught me to play rummy and solitaire. On nights when it was too cold to sit on the porch, we would spend hours playing cards.

I was up at least until midnight these nights. I would sleep with my grandfather because I was terrified to sleep alone. Whenever he would get up in the middle of the night to go to the bathroom, I would have to get up as well and stand on the other side of the door holding the doorknob in order to feel safe. I could be a scared little girl around him, and he never scoffed at me for it.

While around my parents, I had to be a brave little girl and be the interpreter of not only whatever conversations they came across, but also the world around them —such as the mail that they received and the confusion they would have while watching TV. I interpreted the news for them almost daily while I was with them.

I know my grandfather was aware of the responsibilities thrust upon me. He would also rely on me to help with matters with my mother. He was an alcoholic as well, but not an angry, aggressive one, so relying on me was something that couldn't be helped, especially when it came to dealing with my mother. After all, I was the one who could communicate for her.

My mother came through the door one afternoon at my grandfather's house yelling at me immediately. She had hit a girl on a bicycle while driving that day. She was furious with me and said it was my fault because if I had been with her, it wouldn't have happened. My grandfather and I, along with my mother, had to go to the police station to figure out all of the information that she wasn't able to communicate to us. Just another example of normal life for me.

With my grandfather, I was able to be someone who needed to be protected. I could display a kind of vulnerability I couldn't afford to show while caring for my parents. I know that this part of my life was so important. It is a necessity for a child to have someone they feel safe with. Thankfully, I experienced this with my grandfather if only for a while.

When hearing children grow up in a deaf household, not only do the deaf individuals feel unheard but their children do as well. There are so many things unsaid for both parties. Deaf individuals are often frustrated because they are unheard. They don't stop to think that it is possible that they are the ones not hearing their own children's cry for help. Having a loving hearing adult can help tremendously in a situation such as this. I learned about vulnerability because of my grandfather. I didn't know it at the time because I was so young, but lessons that come at a young age are often stored in our subconscious for a later time.

CHAPTER 3

A LONELY GIRL

My grandfather had a stroke when I was eight years old. His whole left side was paralyzed, and he was placed in a nursing home. I was not only devastated because I loved him dearly and never wanted any harm to come to him, but I was also terrified. My one and only protector was not there for me anymore.

My mother refused to go see him. She was going through a hard divorce and drinking more than ever. She was also losing her only other protector besides me. She said she couldn't stand to see him the way he was. It was up to me to get rides to see him. I wasn't going to desert someone who was always there for me. He couldn't speak due to the stroke, but his eyes would light up and he would smile with the right side of his mouth, which was not affected by the incident. The nurses informed me that I was the only person he would react for.

I could even get him to hum along while I sang songs like "You Are My Sunshine" and "Katie Beautiful Lady," and other songs that he had once sung for me while playing his accordion. One day I arrived at the nursing home ready to spend some time with my dear grandpa. I found him having very labored breathing. He couldn't even open his eyes. Other family members were there as well because they had been informed of his condition. At one point, I was the only one in the room with him. I held his finger and asked him to move his finger if he knew I was there. He moved his finger. Just as I was leaving the room, his nurse entered. When she came out, she informed us he had passed. A feeling of helplessness washed over me. How would I ever be able to survive a world of abuse and fear without him by my side?

* * *

My mother's drinking became even worse after her second divorce and the loss of her father. My grandfather had also been her support system. All she had left was her brother, who unfortunately also had a drinking problem. He tried his best to be there for her, but his good intentions would get sidelined by them getting together to go on drinking binges. Whenever they planned to take me someplace, like the zoo or any other outing, I would get my hopes up. I always wanted to believe this time we were going to have a good day. Of course, we would stop at a bar for one drink and end up staying at the bar all night, never arriving at our destination. My heart would sink and my hopes would vanish. But my reward was bags of Vitner's potato chips, Slim Jims, and the dollar bills the patrons would give me to play games.

My mother would often drink very heavily with her brother. He had two children as well. They were nine and ten years older than me. They too had suffered a lot from the effects of alcoholism in their family.

Once, while I was with my father for the weekend, my mother and my uncle had one of their usual nights of going out and getting drunk. My mother was the one to drive them home that night. My uncle had just bought a new Thunderbird and had not yet purchased insurance for it. My mother ran into a pole and totaled the car. Somehow, they both survived the horrific accident. My uncle's family had to continue to make payments on the car because there was no insurance to cover it.

My mother had stitches throughout her mouth, which was swollen to three times its normal size. She also broke her arm. My uncle, who had been asleep in the car, miraculously walked away with no injuries.

I was in church with my father when somebody came and asked us to step out of the service. They explained that they had gotten a phone call and that my mother was in Cook County Hospital. I immediately wanted to leave to be by her side. I knew she desperately needed me.

My father had other ideas. Our church service was not to be interrupted by any situation caused by drinking.

I sat down and tried to hear what the preacher was saying. No matter how I tried, I couldn't concentrate. I felt so anxious my hands were trembling. All I could think about was my mother lying there alone not being able to communicate with the nurses. The service seemed to take five hours to complete. Finally we were able to leave, but only after my father said the proper goodbyes to everyone he knew and loved.

When I arrived at the hospital, I was very anxious. I didn't know what to expect. My mother would mostly place the blame on me whenever things went wrong for her. Her room reeked of blood and alcohol. Her hair was still filled with blood. I couldn't believe my eyes. In a scolding manner, I asked a nurse why my mother wasn't cleaned up. The nurse simply said that was not their main concern, then walked away.

I always had a bit of fear while around my mother, but now her appearance frightened me even more. She looked very scary with her lips so swollen, stitches sticking out of her lips, and blood in her hair. Her arm was in a cast as well. It was a very gruesome sight. But I was responsible for her care, and I did just that. I cared for her through yet another tragedy.

I was able to stay at my father's trailer while she was in the hospital. When she was released, my father agreed to let her stay at his home for a couple of days as well. I was so thankful for that. I needed what little support he could offer. My father was going to pick her up after work, and I waited anxiously all day for her arrival. When she finally walked through the door, my fears were amplified. She still had her hair all knotted up in blood, and she couldn't sign to me much, not only due to her pain but because one of her arms was in a cast. Normally I could understand her speech, even though most people could not. But now, with her lips all stitched up, her speech was even harder to understand. I realized this was going to be harder than I had imagined.

I started out with washing the blood out of her hair. I brushed her hair afterwards so gingerly. The knots in her hair were so tightly bound from days of being soaked in blood and lying in a hospital bed. I then bathed her as well. The smell of blood and body odor that filled the room finally dissipated. I did my best, being ten years old. I then got her settled into the bed in my very small room in my father's trailer.

Those few days were enough for me to get over the fear in my gut of taking care of her while she looked so frightful. When it was time for us to go home, I dreaded the time ahead of us. I knew her bouts of anger would continue and my father wouldn't be there to be the reason she kept it under control. She also had not been drinking during the time in my father's home. That was quickly remedied as soon as we arrived back home. I had a lot of school work to catch up on, as usual. I missed many days of school due to sitting in welfare stations and the social security office to interpret for my mother. These funds were our only means of survival.

Months later, her lips still weren't the same. I was heading out to play one day, and she asked me for a kiss. I rejected the kiss, and she became very angry at me. She slammed a bottle of pills on the table and said she would kill herself. She said no one loved her and she no longer wanted to live. After her death, that was one of many scenes that led to me feeling guilt about her suicide. Guilt is a very strong emotion. It led to me taking on the blame for my mother's years of bad decisions. I was a child, yet I took on the responsibilities of the tragic situations she had put us in.

Many children are taught guilt at an early age. Most do not experience situations as severe as I did, but children's feelings of guilt are real just the same. It is important to not make the same mistakes with our children, and the most important way to do so is to do the work of overcoming the guilt we bury in our souls.

From when I was eight years old until I was thirteen, my mother was very abusive to me. When I wasn't home alone riddled with fear, I would be at some bar with her. She would get so drunk I'm surprised we made it home on the many occasions she drove us home. One night a patron of the bar we were at suggested they drive us home. I begged her to please let them. She was mortified and dragged me to the car, threw me in, and proceeded to beat my chest repeatedly with the hand she wasn't driving with. I was struggling to breathe, and I prayed that a police officer would pull us over. When we arrived home around 3:00 a.m., a relative who was staying with us heard her screaming at me to get out of the car. He forcefully got her into the house, and she passed out shortly after that. He carried me inside and stayed by my side the rest of the night. In the morning I was so sore I could barely breathe. It took a couple of weeks, but I fully recovered.

On another occasion, she picked me up from school intoxicated, with hickeys all over her neck. I panicked. I was embarrassed. I didn't want the teachers, or most of all the other children, to witness this. As if that wasn't humiliating enough, she grabbed me by the hair and started screaming at me. Because she was deaf, her speech sounded very strange to anyone who didn't understand deafness. We got into the car, and she kept screaming at me and hitting me all the way home, which thankfully was only a block away. She passed out shortly after we got home. That beating wasn't as bad as some of the others I received from her, but it was certainly one of the most humiliating.

I went to bed that night thinking about facing the kids at school the next day. I felt so anxious I knew there was no sleep to be had that night. I thought to myself that I could either hang my head in shame or hit the first kid who said anything even remotely close to insulting me. I decided on hitting the first culprit. I figured that if I could take beatings from an enraged adult woman, what kid could possibly hurt me?

So, there he was. I still remember his name. He had blonde hair and would always wear a leather vest. It was a strange look for a ten-year-old child but definitely fitting for a bully. He started mocking the sounds my mother had made while screaming at me the day before. A new anger I didn't recognize rose inside of me. I couldn't hold it in. I punched him in the face. It felt good to me. Afterwards I remember being afraid of how good it felt to me. He hit me back, and my adrenaline kicked in. I didn't feel anything but rage. Some teachers broke it up. I was a girl, so he was the one who got in trouble.

I had fought one of our school's bullies. That earned me respect from some kids, but others saw it as a challenge to fight me. Fortunately, more kids stayed away. I really never wanted to fight. I had enough of that at home. But I did always stick up for the kids getting picked on, and I was prepared to fight for them. I fought a few battles. That wasn't new to me. I had been in survival mode since the age of five.

My mother beat me on many occasions. I often ended up at the hospital when it got to the point where I was so stressed and worn out from the abuse that I would go into convulsions. It would seem my jaw was locked open. Hospitals back in those days didn't do much about child abuse. In fact, they did nothing about it at all.

They would dress my wounds and wrap me in warm blankets. To this day I still remember how the comfort of those warm blankets and warm smiles from nurses soothed me.

My mother would be at my bedside at the hospital. By this time, she was pretty sobered up. I remember falling asleep, and every time I did, she would wake me for fear that I had passed away. She at times would awake in the morning and apologize repeatedly, telling me to go live with my father.

She truly wanted to stop beating me, but the alcohol and the anger always got the best of her. Later in the day, she would beg me to never leave her because she couldn't survive alone. Of course, I never did leave her. If she hadn't left me, I never would have.

Guilt is a strong emotion —maybe one of the strongest. Guilt can cause anxiety, stress, lack of confidence, depression, feelings of worthlessness and more damaging emotions. Overcoming guilt is not an easy feat, and sometimes it requires the help of another who has learned to successfully conquer the emotion. Many times we are carrying around guilt that isn't ours to carry. Guilt is a defeating and worthless emotion. It doesn't help the very situation we are holding the burden of. To overcome guilt is to get a taste of freedom, which is my greatest asset.

CHAPTER 4

CRY FOR HELP

My mother had a string of boyfriends who would come around, mostly when her monthly check came. They would sell our food stamps at one of the local bars for a fraction of their value to purchase alcohol.

Some of these men would try and stick their tongues down my throat and grope me. My stomach would curl; I would push them away and threaten to tell my father. I felt threatened every time a male entered our home.

My beliefs about men formed early on. I was learning what men wanted and expected from women.

Luckily my father was well known in the deaf community. He rode a Harley and was a pretty tough guy. I never did tell him about the abuse at the hands of my mother or her boyfriends. One reason is that I feared he would confront one of these men and get hurt or worse. Maybe he wasn't father of the year, but he treated me much better than my mother did, and I could not risk losing yet another person I loved. Another reason I didn't tell him anything is that I feared he would try to get custody of me. I was only about eleven years old, and I should have done anything to be taken away from the abusive situation I was in, but I knew my mother needed me more than anything. I was her only link to the world. I wrote out the rent checks and managed our social security and welfare money the best I could as a child. When we would get our check, we would pay the rent and what small bills we had, and Mom would spend the rest on drinking.

There was one man I didn't dare tell anyone about. He would come around two or three times a month and would tell me to go to my room and stay there. He would rape my mother, then tell me if I told anyone he would kill us both. I lived with that probably for a year of my life. I would hear my mother crying and screaming in the other room and would stay in my room terrified until the clunking of his boots would signal to me that he was leaving. She would beg me not to tell anyone, and I didn't. He never touched me, but I can still remember every detail of his face.

I'm so grateful that I have learned over the years to train my mind to shift my thoughts. Change your thoughts, change your mind —it is a very valuable lesson to be learned. Perhaps the most important.

Many nights, my mother left me home alone. I was petrified of being alone, but it was less stressful than when she was home finding reasons to be angry with me or having one of her boyfriends around. She looked for excuses to start hitting me when she was drunk. I was thankful for the nights she arrived home too drunk or tired and would just pass out.

On many occasions she would come home bruised up or with a black eye after days of being absent from our home. Once, she told me she had gotten pregnant. I felt the shock well up inside of me, followed by fear. How could she have let this happen? I couldn't imagine her doing to another child what she did to me. How would she ever take care of a baby in her condition?

She decided she would have an abortion. That was a lot to for a twelve-year-old to comprehend. She naturally expected me to go to the clinic with her. When we arrived, we pushed past picketers telling us that we were murderers and we were going to hell. That was one time being deaf benefited her. She didn't have to hear what these people were saying. I'm sure her imagination wasn't as bad as it actually was. I was terrified. Not only did the picketers seem threatening, but I feared for my mother's soul as well.

Abortion clinics don't usually allow children to come in with the patient. I explained to them that my mother was deaf and needed an interpreter, so I was allowed in. I was so uncomfortable sitting in the waiting room after assisting her with all the paperwork. I watched some young girls cry ing while others were nonchalant. I felt the weight of guilt that those people carrying their signs outside had inflicted upon me. I had assisted in terminating the pregnancy that would have been my little brother or sister. I felt so ashamed inside.

My mother didn't learn any lessons from that experience. In no time, she was back to her ways of partying until all hours of the night and sometimes for days. Not long after the abortion experience, she came home to wake me and tell me she had been raped. She was wearing a tampon at the time. Once again, I was expected to come along and be her voice and translator.

We headed to the hospital. I explained the situation, and she was treated. I was exhausted, as I often was, being a child taking care of a parent. I missed more school. It is a wonder that I was able to maintain a passing grade point average in grammar school with no guidance and such bad attendance. I was very smart and tested well.

My childhood wasn't really a childhood at all. I was an adult way before my time. One day when a friend had come over to see the new stereo my father had bought me, the friend asked, " Don't you have any toys?" I never really thought about it until then, but I didn't. My savior was that stereo. I would play music and dance. The feeling I felt while dancing lifted me above all the pain and sadness. It aligned me with the emotion of joy. I felt so free. I spent many hours dreaming of being a dancer. I spent hours choreographing dances. I still love to dance around the house to my favorite songs. Dancing is very therapeutic, and I highly recommend it. I'm not sure why as adults we lose touch with some of the remedies we used as children to feel better. Watch a child, and you can learn so much from them.

Sad songs helped me feel relief as well. I felt if people were writing sad songs, then others must be hurting as well. I felt it was a common thing feeling sad. I didn't feel so alone while listening to them.

I had so many behaviors and habits then that nowadays would be labeled as ADHD or OCD. I not only got over these behaviors on my own, but I also achieved a successful life as well. That's one of the reasons I am against giving medication to children before exhausting every other way of teaching them coping skills and other ways of expressing themselves.

I had a best friend who would sometimes spend the night. Most of the time my mother wasn't home, but we would lie to her parents and say she was. Most of the time they didn't check because my mother was deaf, and most people didn't go out of their way to talk to her. On many occasions my mother would come home and beat me while my friend was still over. I would tell my friend to just stay in my room no matter what. She was terrified, rightfully so, but through it all we remained friends for many years. That friend was there through most of the trauma in my life, and I am very grateful for the time of our friendship. Friends can be an amazing way to cope and get through tough situations.

Never underestimate the power of friendship. Being in the life situation I was in, I could have pushed people away due to embarrassment or anger. It's important to be open to letting people in your life while keeping the predators at bay. It's even more important to be able to know the difference between the two types of people.

* * *

My time spent with my mother was filled with her repeatedly telling me that I was the cause of her hardships, her failed marriage and relationships, basically all her unhappiness. After her suicide, you can imagine the guilt I felt for not being able to save her. In her very rare times of being sober, she would tell me she was sorry and that I should go live with my father while at the same time begging me not to leave her.

At twelve years old, I started drinking with kids who hung out at the school ground. I smoked weed and started smoking cigarettes. I started to rebel. I would pull out a pack of cigarettes and a beer right in front of my mother. She would go into her fits, but I was showing her what she was, and I didn't care anymore. I didn't act this way while I was away for the weekend with my father. I was just doing it to hurt my mother who was always hurting me. It wasn't long before the Simon City Royals, a neighborhood gang, started hanging around my apartment building. They would tell me to go ahead inside and get some sleep. They would be sitting outside partying and making sure I was safe while my mother was gone. That was the beginning of my partying days. I was always stoned or drunk.

On my thirteenth birthday, my mother surprised me by having a party for me. She had a cake with elephants on them. I loved and collected elephants. She was present and sober for the party. She had trick candles on the cake, and I remember her holding my hair back after it almost started on fire because I wasn't expecting the candles to light again. The joy of having my mother present and seeming to enjoy time spent with me was priceless. I don't have many pleasant memories of her, so I treasure the ones I have.

Christmas that year was equally amazing. She had so many presents for me. I don't really remember all the gifts she gave me, but what I do remember is she could barely contain her excitement. She kept giving me gifts a couple of weeks prior to the actual day. The excitement I experienced from her made me feel so loved. That was a rare feeling for me. I thought maybe things were going to improve after all. Little did I know it was my last Christmas with her. I'm pretty sure she knew.

My father was pretty good about coming to get me most weekends, unless he was in a relationship with a woman. I then would be out on the back burner for a few months to a year. He married someone when he was forty. She was eighteen and pregnant. The marriage didn't even last as long as the pregnancy did. They gave up their son, my little brother, for adoption.

He ended up finding me long after my father had passed, and I'm so glad he did. He is also deaf, and a very sweet addition to my life.

As hurt and abused children, we often become the very thing that is hurting us. Maybe we do it to make sense of it all, or to understand why it is being done unto us. For me, the fighting and partying were also a way of getting even. I wanted to show that I was in control. Actually, these actions are a sure way to spin out of control, but when you're young and no one is listening it's the only thing that makes sense.

If you know a child who is acting out, please do not label that child as bad or anything else negative. They are demonstrating a cry for help. Sometimes traditional help only makes them rebel more. It really helps to get help from a mentor or someone who has experienced what they are going through and can relate and talk to them on their level.

CHAPTER 5

A NEW FAMILY

After the passing of my mother, I moved in with my father. He was engaged to be married. He asked me if I was okay with the marriage. I was trying to cope with what had just happened to me. I also was dealing with being the new kid in the family. I wanted him all to myself, but I of course wanted him to be happy and didn't think anything could ever be worse than what I had already been through. Being as mature as I was, I told him to please do what made him happy. They'd had a daughter together seven years prior. She deserved a father and a family life. Her mother and my father broke up shortly after she was born, and they reconnected seven years later and decided it was time to unite. Now they were getting married, and I dreamed of being a part of a real family. We were planning a wedding! I was still grieving the loss of my mother and working through all the guilt and emotional pain from all the abuse, but I had hope for the first time in a long time.

My father was a minister for the deaf at the Church of Christ, and that's where the wedding took place. It was a small ceremony and simply decorated, but lovely.

During the reception that followed, everyone seemed happy. I started to feel a wave of guilt for feeling happy, so I stepped outside for a breath of air. My new stepmother followed me outside. She began to talk about my cat that I had brought along with me to my father's home when I moved in. She had told me previously that when they got married and we moved into our new double-wide trailer, I could keep my cat. Well, she couldn't even wait until we got home after the occasion to tell me that she would not be allowing me to keep my cat. I felt as though I was punched in the gut. The heat from the sun suddenly felt unbearable. I couldn't even reply, I was so shocked. I ran in to tell my father, but it was his wedding day so of course he said we would talk about it later. Later that evening, he explained that the cat made my stepmother unhappy, so it had to go. That was the beginning of her mistreatment towards me and the beginning of me losing the hope I had dared to feel.

Within the first week I was beginning to witness some unkind behavior toward me. One day I could smell the delicious aroma of my stepmother cooking salmon patties, and I was looking forward to a home-cooked meal. My father wasn't much of a cook, and my mother had never provided adequate meals. I sat down at the table antici-pating a family meal. She passed out plates to everyone but me. I didn't want to ask her to serve me, so I got up and made myself a plate and sat down. She grabbed my plate and put it in the sink. This prompted an argument between my father and my stepmother. My father placed the plate back in front of me, and she got up and stormed off to their bedroom. I didn't know what to do. My father instructed me and my little sister to eat, then ran after her. I had pretty much lost my appetite, and I went to my room.

I was feeling so much disappointment and confusion. I didn't know what I had done wrong. I just knew that my hope for a loving family environment was diminishing fast. Many more incidents continued to take place for weeks and months to come. If I sat down in the living room to watch TV with the family, she would run for their bedroom with the noise of a slamming door to follow.

Christmas came, and I had managed to get a little something for everyone, including my stepmother. I was reminiscing about the past Christmas with my mother. I was feeling sad about how things could have been if my mother would have chosen to get help. I also was determined to do my part to try and fix the dysfunction in my new family life. My little sister was excited and went in our parents' room to wake them to begin to open presents. The tree was beautiful and filled with gifts with pretty wrapping and bows. I passed out my small trinkets of thoughtful gifts to each one of them. My stepmother did not open hers. My father thanked me politely for his money clip that said *#1 Dad*, and my sister was so excited to open all her gifts. After all was said and done, there wasn't even one gift under that tree for me. I felt so hurt. It really wasn't about receiving gifts for me; I was used to not having much. But the feeling of being so insignificant was almost unbearable.

I was deeply saddened that my father didn't feel it was important to get a gift for me. My little sister had more gifts than you could count. My eyes filled with tears, and I met my father's gaze with just enough time for him to see them. I grabbed my coat and walked about two miles to my friend's house. She had a gift for me. It was Michael Jackson's *Thriller* album. She may as well have given me ten pounds of gold. I was so deeply touched. I can still recall the feeling I had. I hung out with her family that whole day. I have many fond memories of my friend Marsha. She was a blessing to have as a friend during those times.

* * *

I didn't see my paternal grandmother very much while my mother was alive. On my weekends with my father we would sometimes pop in to say hello to her, but she and I were never close. After my mother's passing, we began a new chapter and started to get to know each other. I would spend some weekends with her. It was a great escape. She was in my corner as best as she could be. I did look forward to spending time with her. I was able to be a child with her. I learned about planting gardens, flowers, and God. She didn't attend church, but she taught me about a loving God who didn't judge so harshly but rather loved us and looked out for us. Those teachings could have been what saved my life when I went through some really horrific experiences that were awaiting me in my near future. We would do fun things like singing "Fish Heads" and waking in the middle of the night to eat egg sandwiches.

I loved her, but of course didn't always want to be hanging around my grandmother. I wanted friends and a teenage life. When I went through hard times, she would remind me to keep my faith. She was old school and taught me a lot about discipline. She also would say things to me that would further diminish my confidence, such as "There will always be a girl better, prettier, and smarter than you." When she said thing along those lines, I felt it deep in my soul, and it hurt deeply and sometimes still does. She said these things to me so I would know how to take care of my husband in the future, whoever he might be.

My paternal grandmother became someone I loved and adored. I thought I finally had someone I could trust one hundred percent. I did during those times, thankfully. She gave me a foundation and I believe tools to overcome and get through some experiences that most do not conquer. She had five children and was in an abusive marriage. She left him with five little children in tow. She was only twenty-two years old. She remarried and prevailed against all odds. She instilled some of that strength in me, and I'm forever grateful. She won some battles against my stepmother. She talked my father into getting me braces, and some necessities once in a while. I would call her from time to time while I was a runaway. She would tell me she understood and to have faith in God. What else could she do? I was becoming an out-of-control teenager. I knew she loved me, though, and that was something.

To my father's credit, he tried to argue for my rights as his daughter. But I would tell him not to fight. I would just leave our trailer. This began a series of late nights out, hanging with older kids who really didn't have families they had to go home to either. Drinking and smoking pot became daily habits. I really didn't want to be behaving this way, but what choice did I have? I wanted friends, and I didn't have to feel ashamed around these friends. They were like me: escaping a dysfunctional home.

I was a young girl who wanted to be good. I was being challenged from every angle. The good kids were home with their families. I didn't have a family. The kids without healthy families became my family. The partying was kind of fun at first, and it did help me forget the pain for a while. Substance abuse creeps up on you. It is a way of connecting with others who are suffering, and it becomes a way of finding laughter and fun in a place of crying and darkness. It is a deceiving situation. The very thing you think is giving you relief is really destroying you. I am so thankful that I have chosen to fight the battle and kick those vices out of my life. It's not an easy task, and it requires a lot of self-discipline. It comes with learning how to heal the hurt. For me it was learning to change my mindset. I studied a lot about that over many years, and now I help others take control of their thoughts and become aware of their emotional scale.

CHAPTER 6

THE ULTIMATE SACRIFICE

When I was thirteen, I started working for a local small convenience store there in Hegewisch. I would visit this store daily after school with some friends. There were video games there, so it was a popular spot for kids.

The owner must have had a knack for spotting vulnerable children. He offered me a job as a cashier. My father barely gave me lunch money due to my stepmother's fits, so I of course jumped at the offer. He paid me $10 a day cash and a pack of cigarettes. I would start after school and stay until around 8:00 p.m. I was proud to be thirteen years old and working. I ate fast food and had lunch money every day with that $10. I saved my change to do laundry at a laundromat at the end of each week. I was grateful to say the least. I had a job and worked in an environment where I could see my friends daily. The owner complimented me often and made me feel cared for as well.

Then came the day that, yet again, an adult who I trusted showed me their true colors. He asked me if I would clean the meat slicer in the back room. I of course said yes and went on my way to do so. As I started to clean the slicer, he came into the room with a look on his face I had not seen before. He began to molest me. I could smell the dirty dish rag on the counter, and I just tried to concentrate on anything other than what was happening. I had learned from my mother's beatings to try and place myself somewhere else in my mind. That was the beginning of my learning that we have control over our minds. I didn't realize at the time that I was learning a valuable lesson. It is truly one of my greatest gifts in life today. I still make sure I switch out my kitchen washcloths out frequently. I hate to smell a dirty dish rag. It brings back memories of the days of being molested.

Afterwards he composed himself and went up front to the register. I was left there to try and understand what had just happened. My friend, my boss, the source of my being able to have a bit of money and independence, had just shattered my world. I stood there bewildered for a moment. I then straightened up and composed myself as well as I could. I proceeded to clean the meat slicer and headed to the front of the store afterwards. My stomach was very nauseous, and I felt a bit unsteady while facing him. I didn't know what to expect. He said thank you for cleaning the slicer. He then acted as nothing had happened. He laughed and joked with me like we always had. This became a daily ritual. Cleaning the meat slicer was code for his ten minutes a day of pleasure and my ten minutes a day of complete horror. People don't understand why sometimes women stay in abusive relationships. I do. For me, the reason was that my abuser was the only adult friend who seemed to care for me and help me. Sometimes the abuser is the victim's only friend or source of wellbeing.

Aside from that portion of the day, he was kind and concerned (or so it seemed) about my well being. I continued to work for him for two years.

During those two years, there were of course regulars who would hang out at the store. I got to know many of them and chatted with a lot of the neighbors who frequently came in. One in particular was a charming twenty-five-year-old man. He had a smile that could crawl into your heart, grab hold and not let go. At least that was what it did to my heart. I began to long for the door to open and to see him walk in. He paid a lot of attention to me and took the time to chat with me before or after his time on the video games.

He started to be there when it was closing time, and we would walk around the neighborhood. We would sit at the park down the street and talk about what we wanted in life, and everything else under the sun.

Then it happened: he kissed me. I thought I flew right up to heaven. It wasn't the first time I had been kissed by a boy. In fact, I was dating someone at the time, but he was a high school boy with a good family. I felt I wasn't in his league. I lived in the trailer court, and no one ever knew about my daily chore in the back of that convenience store. I was still a virgin despite the molestation I encountered on almost a daily basis. I started hanging out with the twenty-five-year-old more and more. I started hanging at his trailer that he lived with his mother in. Why his mother didn't say anything about a fifteen-year-old girl hanging out at the trailer with him at his age is beyond me. I was in my glory. He seemed to be falling in love with me, and I thought I was head over heels in love with him.

Then it happened. He asked me if I thought I was old enough and ready to have sex with him. If not, he would have to find another girlfriend. I didn't want to lose him, so of course I said I was ready, but I was concerned about getting pregnant. He told me he was sterile and couldn't get me pregnant. I of course hung on every word he said, so I agreed.

It happened. Afterwards I wrapped myself in a blanket and walked to the bathroom and cried. He followed me in and sat and consoled me. I felt somewhat safe with him. After that we made love quite a bit. I became more and more comfortable with the act. We had fun together. He had me quit working at the convenience store and spend all my time at his trailer with him. We would play cards, listen to Kool and the Gang, dance together, and eat a lot of mac and cheese and hot dogs. I was happy and was glad to be out of that store. I would still go in and chat with the owner. After all, he was my friend in my mind. I had never known anything but some sort of abuse from people who loved me, so I felt it was normal. We no longer had our time in the backroom, and I was so relieved that it was easier for me to be in his presence.

I was barely making it to school, and no one including the school staff seemed to care. The man I was living with wanted me to run away with him. I had to come up with a plan, because although I knew my family members wouldn't come looking for me, the school might miss me if I never showed up at all.

I knew it wouldn't be hard to convince my father to help me leave school. It would certainly make his life easier and less complicated. If I came up with a good reason, it would even ease his sense of guilt, so I knew he would jump at the chance. I explained to him that the school wanted to send me to a special school out of the state to enhance my interpreting skills. All he had to do was go to my current school and sign the papers. This made sense to him; after all, I was his interpreter. When we arrived there, I told the staff that my father was there to sign transfer papers because we were moving. But my father could not hear me saying that.

I learned at an early age that most people do not want to communicate with people who make them uncomfortable. In that day and age, I believe most people found deaf people a little unnerving, the way they spoke strangely and signed. At least, that was my experience. That might be part of the reason why my deception worked. The staff were probably just glad I was there to interpret, and they did not ask questions. I was free of school and very happy to be. I tested above average and was a smart child, but I never fit in with any of the crowds at school.

Now that I didn't have to worry about school, I was free to move in with my boyfriend. We moved in with some friends in the trailer court first. I remember some of the people, mostly by first name only, and I basically went along with whatever was happening every day. There was an older man and his son. He owned a school bus; we lived with him and a few other friends. They were all young men. I was the only female. I was also pregnant. I was beginning to realize that my boyfriend, along with not being sterile, was also telling me many lies. He also began to hit me now and then when I didn't agree with him or go along with something he said to do. He hit me much less than my mother had, so in my mind it wasn't so bad.

The older man we lived with seemed to have quite a bit of money despite living in a trailer. One evening he said we should all go get a bite to eat. He told us to bring along all our laundry, and our cartons of cigarettes as well. He also had us bring along our pet, a Doberman puppy. We thought it was strange that he was telling us to bring all these things just to go get a bite to eat, but we didn't question him. We piled into the school bus and were on our way. There were five of us.

Upon our arrival home after dinner, the trailer we had been living in was burned to the ground. I was in shock, but even at fifteen years old I knew that he'd told us to bring along some of our belongings because he was in on the trailer being set on fire. I was heartbroken —not because where we were staying had been destroyed, but rather because my stereo was gone. My stereo was my friend. It had gotten me through all the rough times I'd lived through up until this point. It was my prized possession. Well, my only possession.

The man we were living with informed us that we would be leaving for Florida. I couldn't have cared less where we were going. I had nothing to leave behind. My boyfriend started getting addicted to downers and was getting more and more comfortable with hitting me. On our way to

Florida, we stayed at hotels some nights and slept in the bus some nights. I knew I had to get out. I started to realize that the man we were traveling with was not a good man, nor was my boyfriend.

I no longer had just me to think about. I had to think about my baby growing inside of me. I was used to abuse and quite frankly thought it was a normal part of life, but I knew I didn't want that for my child.

I called my paternal grandmother. She was understandably upset to find out I was pregnant, but she allowed me to live with her. After talking with me about the possibilities of abortion and not being successful with that option, she arranged for my baby to be given up for adoption. She was a crossing guard and knew a lot of people, and she told me she knew of a lawyer and his wife who couldn't have children and they had longed for one for so long. She explained to me that my baby would be so loved and cared for. This couple had a loving marriage and were financially secure.

At first, I fought the decision. I didn't want to give up a part of myself I could love and take care of. After some time, I came to realize I couldn't live with my grandmother with a baby. She was over seventy years old. I thought long and hard about it and realized that at fifteen years old I couldn't provide a baby with a stable home and all the necessities he or she would require.

Living with my grandmother during my pregnancy was challenging for sure. I loved her very much and deeply appreciated her help. I did feel isolated and alone while being pregnant. Many of my old friends wouldn't speak to me, and when I would go to Hegewisch to hang out for a day, many would stare and whisper, and I felt humiliated. Thank God for the true friends who stuck by my side and helped me keep my head up. Marsha was one of those friends, and I am forever grateful. My friend Sue was there for me as well. She was the friend who would stay the night at my mother's apartment and had witnessed some of the abuse. She lived on the north side of Chicago. I was so independent, and no one really missed me much when I was gone, so I would spend weekends in Hegewisch, and even a whole summer after the baby was born.

My grandmother was old-fashioned and kept telling me I was eating for two and continued to harp on me to keep eating beyond what I wanted to eat. I started to overeat on my own out of sheer boredom. I gained nearly a hundred pounds during this time, which was the beginning of my unhealthy relationship with food which lasted for years. I have been all over the scale, from almost two hundred pounds to eighty pounds.

The time arrived. I was two weeks late and finally in labor. My aunt was in from California. She drove with us to the hospital. I had no idea what to expect. My aunt tried to stay in the room with me but started hyperventilating due to stress, so she had to leave. I was alone and terrified. My father walked into the room. I was shocked and filled with so many emotions at seeing him there. He took my hand, and his eyes filled with tears. I felt loved but also guilty and ashamed. I always knew my father loved me, but this was a very moving experience. He had to leave as well. He said it was too hard to see me in such pain. I kept yelling to the nurses that I was having terrible pains and I had to push. I have great respect for nurses, but one nurse said something I felt was unkind: "It didn't hurt going in, did it?" Another nurse came in and said it would be a while, since it was my first child. I said, " Please, I'm having this baby right now." She checked me and said, "Oh my God, I can see the head."

In those days, hospitals prepped you in one room, then took you to the delivery room just before delivery. They were panicked as they got me onto a gurney. I tried to focus on the sound the wheels were making as they wheeled me into the delivery room. I was trying anything to distract myself from the complete fear I was feeling. I was alone and thinking, *When it comes down to it, all I have is me.* I delivered so quickly that the doctor came in after he was born. A nurse yelled out, " It's a boy!" Then there were some muffled words exchanged, and they whisked him away. My heart felt as though it had shattered into a million pieces and I would never be okay again. The nurses took me to the room where I was expected to stay at least two nights for observation. I insisted on being discharged as soon as possible. I delivered him around five a.m. and was let go that evening. I couldn't bear to be there knowing he was somewhere nearby and I couldn't see him. A couple of days later, I had to go back. Indiana state laws insisted that I hold him and hand him over. I thought I couldn't feel any deeper pain than childbirth, but I was wrong. Holding him even for a few seconds was unbearable. My aunt went with me. She was a wonderful person who was always loving and positive. It was too bad she lived so far away from me. I loved her very much. When they took him out of my arms, I felt as though they had ripped my heart out along with him. I buried my head in my aunt's shoulder and cried harder than I ever had before.

That was about the time I vowed no one would ever get close enough to hurt me again.

This was the beginning of my learning how to put up walls, and when I lost what was left of my innocence. I have come a long way in regaining the ability to trust. That is not to say it comes easily to me, but I can actually be vulnerable now. I guess that's obvious since I am writing this book. I am telling my story in hopes of helping many who cannot. Self- love, love for others, and the ability to love life again —these things are possible for everyone.

CHAPTER 7

A LONG ROAD TO INDEPENDENCE

After the birth of my child, I moved around a bit. I tried living with one family member, but I wasn't really safe there. I was raped by a frequent visitor. I was sleeping on the couch when he let himself in and approached me. There were no adults present, just small children who were asleep in their rooms. I was so afraid. I wasn't afraid for my life, as I knew this person would not hurt me physically. He was just another alcoholic who could not control their actions while intoxicated. I was afraid because I didn't want the children to wake up and see what was happening, knowing that he was so inebriated that he would not stop even if one of them walked in. I felt cold and alone and had already begun to learn how to place myself somewhere else while in an abusive situation. I tried without any success to push him off of me. He was much stronger and bigger than I was. If I screamed, no one but the kids would hear me. He made sure to keep my mouth muffled anyway. I had already been abused so much that I knew how to just wait and anticipate the end of the current abusive situation. My biggest fear did come true, and one of the kids woke up. Many years later, she brought it up to me and we talked a bit about it, but we never brought it up again.

I didn't tell the family members I was living with about the rape. I knew they would not believe me or even care. They never failed to remind me that I was lucky to be living with them. I moved out the following week.

* * *

I was back at my dad' s trying to go back to school after the adoption of my son. They still had no interest in me coming home and made it clear that I was just a bother to have around. My stepmother was still arguing about my presence and not wanting me to eat any of their food. I often lived with friends here or there.

I was still getting in trouble. One example was the night before Thanksgiving. I was hanging out with my best friend at the time and her boyfriend in Hegewisch. He had a car, so we were cruising around and finding fields to plow through and empty parking lots so he could do dough-nuts with his car. For those of you who have never heard of the term, it means accelerating your car, then braking just enough while turning the steering wheel to spin in circles with your car.

I'm sure he was trying to impress us. He had an old Chevy Impala. Well, I never was too impressed by guys and their boasting. I was always thinking in my head, *If you can do that, so can I.* Well, of course I asked him if I could try. It was probably the third time I'd ever driven. Surprisingly I picked up on how to spin doughnuts pretty quickly. It was getting close to 10:00 p.m. My friend Laurie had to get home because normal families demanded their children be in at a decent time. She lived in the same trailer court I lived in —just down the block, in fact. We dropped her off, then proceeded to my place. But I looked at Felix and said, "Hey, I don't need to be home; let's keep cruising." He was older than us and had no curfew to adhere to.

I said, "I want to drive, though." He was game, and I drove all over and did a few more doughnuts. I was feeling pretty confident about my driving skills.

Did I mention we were getting high throughout this whole evening?

So finally, he decided we'd better get home.

We were around the corner from my father's trailer, and I decided I could do a burnout —another move Felix taught me that night with his car. I pressed on the brake, accelerated, made a loud screeching noise, and off I went. But I lost control of the car. Earlier, Felix had said to me, "If you hit anything. . . keep going." Well, the back end swerved into a small light post and knocked it over, along with knocking the front end off of a neighbor's Chevy Nova. Then our car plowed across the street and hit a Cadillac and then a Lincoln, slamming them into the neighbor's trailer. Why such expensive cars would be in a trailer park was beyond me, but I guess they had guests over to celebrate Thanksgiving the next day. The people who lived in that part of the trailer court considered themselves better than the trailer owners across the street. Our side had new double-wide trailers, and they were done up nice.

Anyway, here I was in a car that was pretty smashed up, and I looked over and Felix was knocked out. I thought he was dead. I ran out of the car and went across the street to my father's trailer and was frantically ringing the doorbell. The lights in the trailer flashed to inform my deaf parents that the doorbell was being rung. My dad came to the door, and I was crying and trying my best to convey what had just happened. My little sister was awakened by all the commotion and came to the door. I said, "I think I killed Felix." I was sobbing. A few minutes later, Felix walked in the door, and right behind him were the neighbors whose cars and home I'd just destroyed.

I was never so happy to see someone. Felix was okay. We all went outside, and my father said, "You did this?" I said yes. He shook his head with such disappointment I will never forget.

When the police arrived, my dad just said " Take them away" and went back to bed. The police put Felix and me in the back of the squad car, and off we went.

I looked at Felix and said, "Try not to worry. This won't last forever. It will work itself out." But he was too angry with me to even look at me. Of course he wasn't taking any responsibility for allowing a minor to drive his car.

Well, the police couldn't put me in a cell because I wasn't old enough. They allowed me to make a call. I called my cousin Johnny. He lived on the north side of Chicago. It was probably around 1:30 or 2:00 in the morning.

He drove all the way to the south side to come get me. He is a very good person who had enough on his plate taking care of his own family's dysfunction, but he came to get me. I'll never forget the lecture he gave me on that long drive back to his house. I probably acted like I wasn't listening and couldn't have cared less, but actually his words got through to me and I knew I wanted a better life than just goofing off and ending up in police stations. I still tease him to this day about the "long " lecture, but in my heart I truly appreciate it. He is very dear to me, and we are still close and hang out often. He is someone who I look forward to being around. I'm always smiling and happy around him.

My father was responsible for $1,500 in damages. Maybe it was the deductible of their insurance; I'm not sure. I had to go to court with my father. He worked for the city, in the Department of Streets and Sanitation in Edward Vrdolyak's ward, and he knew the alderman. The alderman's brother represented me in court. My case was dismissed, and I kept my nose semi-clean after that.

I felt I had to do something to get my life on track if I ever wanted a future.

I tried moving back in with my father. I was determined to make things work with my stepmother. My goal was to go back to school and get my life together. My stepmother was still as ornery as ever. I needed money to take the bus to school and back. My father would argue with her about it every week, and some weeks she would win the argument. Those were the days that I would hitchhike to school. I stayed in school for a short while, but my dysfunctional home life and my love of smoking pot got in the way. I dropped out. This time I was of age to do so.

Although I had one or two good grammar school friends in Hegewisch, they had good families and had to be in at a decent hour. I started hanging with a group of kids whose parents didn't care that they were out all hours of the night, as I'd started to be. I also would go to my old neighborhood. This was the summer I stayed in friends' basements and hid out all summer. I didn't have to put too much effort into hiding. No one really wanted to find me.

That summer was filled with drinking and smoking a lot of pot. I was sixteen years old and already well on my way to learning quickly what partying was all about. I thought I was having the time of my life. No rules, no one telling me what to do. I felt so cool hanging with the older kids. They seemed to like me and accepted me in their fold. They were filling a void of needing to be loved, cared for and accepted. When the summer ended, surprisingly my father came looking for me. He said my grandmother was worried and I needed to come home. Off I went, back to the south side and the trailer courts.

A few months prior, while I was still pregnant, I was sitting at a school ground and this handsome kid named Jay came up to me and asked my name. I stood up and said, "Look, I'm pregnant. So why don't you just go away?"

He was around eighteen years old. He replied, "What are you so mad about? Don't you want a friend?"

Well, he stuck around and made me laugh. After moving back to Hegewisch I found out he was an older brother of one of my friends. He had just gotten out of a detention center when I met him. He was so handsome and funny, and he could charm anyone with his long hair and outgoing personality.

Some months later, I was staying the night at his house, being as I was his sister's friend. He came home in the middle of the night and knocked on her door to have me join him in having a few beers. I was still considerably overweight from having my baby. He made me feel beautiful. He looked me right in the eyes and with a big grin on his face told me how beautiful I was. Looking back into his big blue eyes, I would have believed anything he told me. I learned sometime after that night that believing him was safe to do. He told me loved me, and to this day I believe he did. I knew I loved him. This is a time in my life I can still recall almost every moment. I can still see every curve of his face, his smile, and his characteristics. I still cherish my memories of Jay. I sure learned a lot from him that helped me cope. You see, he needed to cope as well.

Although Jay was never faithful to me as a boyfriend, he never lied to me. He always told me he was unfaithful and that he loved me, but he was not the type of person to be faithful. He still treated me like a queen when we were together and made me laugh. I felt safe with him. We spent many nights together dancing on the hood of his mother's car or hanging out on picnic benches by the lake on the East Side. We would "
borrow" people's canoes late in the night and be out on the water talking for hours. He always put me first, even if he'd see me while walking down the street holding another

girl's hand. . . he would drop her hand and run up to me with so much love and sweetness.

Yes, it broke my heart when I knew he was with someone else. He even cheated on me with my best friend at the time. She did not (for obvious reasons) stay my best friend for long.

But what did I know about being treated right? Anyone who had ever said they loved me up until this point had always hurt me. Jay at least was honest and protected me from anyone who ever showed any possibility of hurting me. My baby's father came looking for me at Jay's house once, but Jay was not going to allow him to see me or hurt me anymore. I had never had anyone other than my grandmother stand up for me.

I felt extremely lucky that Jay spent time with me. He made me feel like the most important person in the world while I was with him. I still respect him for his brutal honesty. It taught me that we cannot blame anyone for the way they treat us if we choose to stay in that relationship. And I mean any relationship. No one can treat us any way unless we allow it. Taking responsibility for our actions is the first step to healing.

To this day I stress to anyone in my life the importance of being truthful to me. I can forgive anything if the person is truthful about what they did. I then get to choose whether I want to keep them in my circle depending on what the act was. I have high standards for anyone being a part of my life these days. That comes with learning self-worth —an absolutely necessary lesson to learn if you want to overcome and succeed in life. I no longer will allow infidelity or any type of abuse in my relationships.

Jay is still a huge part of my heart, and I smile when I think of him.

I was not an adult at this point, but I sure had already been through more than most adults by that time. Even with Jay being unfaithful to me, I made the decision of continuing a relationship with him but also seeing other people as well. I chose to be honest with them like Jay was to me. I always talked about how much I loved Jay and would take any opportunity to be with him if it arose. I wouldn't see him for days, weeks sometimes. He always came back around, and I was always so excited to see him. Anyone who knew me knew I loved Jay. He would get very upset knowing I was dating others but understood that he was doing the same and couldn't expect more from me.

One evening he came to my trailer's bedroom window. I heard his familiar knock and happily jumped out of bed to see him. He was standing there with his friend, whom I was seeing as well. I have to admit I saw other boys just to upset him. It verified for me that he cared. He seemed more upset than usual that I was seeing someone else as well. He gave me an ultimatum. It was him or his friend. I then became angry as well and told him that when he gave up others, so would I. He punched my father's shed, and his hand looked pretty messed up and he was bleeding. He ran off, and I was devastated, I didn't see him for weeks and kept asking around for him. There weren't any cell phones or beepers back then. Finally, I was told that he and that same friend he showed up to my house with had gotten arrested that night. I called every facility and finally found him. I was informed on how to write a letter to an inmate.

He went away for two years for robbing homes. Thank God he never hurt anyone. I don't believe he ever could. Every day I checked the mail for any letter from him. When I received one, I would cry tears of joy, but many days I cried tears of anguish. I was staying at my father's trailer again, dealing with the mistreatment from my stepmother, and the one person who brought me some happiness was locked away from me.

His friend was writing me as well, but the letters from Jay were all I could think of —all that mattered to me.

I'm not justifying what he did. I guess I'm just justifying the fact that I loved somebody who went to jail.

I was sending him letters daily and money when I could. I thought I was the only one writing him and taking care of him. It made me proud. I felt he would finally see that I was the one who cared for him, the one he would come home to and be faithful to. Of course, I learned that other girls were also sending him letters and money, believing they were the ones he was coming home to eventually. I was counting the days until I turned eighteen. That was when I could visit him. I lived for the days I could get a ride to Joliet prison see him. Sometimes my father would even take me. I guess he could see how much I loved Jay and cared for him.

I had a cousin, Diane, who would come to visit me periodically. She was the daughter of my mother's brother.

She and her brother were the only family members from my mother's side of the family that took the time to even care where I may have ended up. She had grown up in a dysfunctional home as well. She had acquired a life of serious addiction due to it. It eventually took her life, but not before robbing her of all her joy and happiness. She was nine years older than me. She was beautiful inside and out; anyone who met her loved her instantly. She was such a caring soul. I hated what drugs had done to her, and although I'd had my share, it was her example that kept me from going too far. She worked at a large factory in Franklin Park. When I turned eighteen, she told me she could get me hired on there. I was so excited. It was a good- paying union job. With nothing more than a tank of gas, I drove away without looking back.

I managed to get an apartment on the north side of Chicago. My first night there, I looked around and couldn't believe I had my own place. I was afraid but determined to make a home for myself.

All I had was a cot and a bar stool I stole from the Chicago game room.

I slowly prepared the place to be ready for Jay. He would be getting out in a few months. I was now finally getting my life together aside from too much drinking and smoking weed. Many days I would sleep in the parking lot because I was out partying too late. I was always in control, though. I held that job for six years and always paid my bills on time. One thing I had learned from taking care of my deaf parents was how to be responsible.

The time came when Jay was released from prison. I received a phone call from him. The one I dreamed about nearly every night was coming home. There was a new feeling inside of me: pride. Not only had I managed to get hired at a huge company, I passed my trial period, bid on a better position, and got it. I bought a Mustang and was doing a damn good job of taking care of myself. When Jay came to stay with me, it only took me a couple of days to start realizing that this probably wasn't a good idea. I would even take my landline phone to work with me because I knew otherwise he would be calling other girls. Now that I was working and obtaining my own things I was no longer willing to accept that I wasn't the only one. He swore up and down that I would be the only one, but not long after that he made a pass at my best friend. That was the end of Jay and me. It tore me up inside, but for the first time I had confidence and knew I deserved better, and I vowed if any hurting was going to be going on, I would be the one doing it.

Much later, when I was around thirty years old and newly divorced, Jay somehow got hold of my phone number and called me. He wanted to meet me after all these years. I of course agreed to it. He was married, but that never stopped Jay. I would not engage in any romantic relationship with him, mainly because by that time I had two little children whom I never wanted to expose to that part of my life. I met him at Navy Pier. I was sitting on his lap reminiscing over our young years. A stranger came up to us with a Polaroid camera and insisted on taking a picture of us. She handed

it to me and said, " One day you will cherish this photo."
Jay passed away shortly after that. The stranger was correct.

* * *

My father came to visit me in my new apartment almost a
year later. He and my stepmother were getting a divorce.
This began a new relationship with my father like I'd never
had previously. I finally had him back as a father. He visited
me frequently throughout the years before he died. I had
the chance to get close to him again.

I had a new life, a new place to live, and I believed all
was well. For the most part it was. I met a new guy and of
course let him move in. I supported him throughout his
schooling to become an auto body repairman. We were
happy. We even got engaged. I developed an addiction to
cocaine while in that relationship. I was also battling an
eating disorder, which, in my mind, cocaine helped with.
I was down to eighty pounds. I would get on the scale and
think, " Just ten more pounds to lose." I was deteriorating.
You see, when you go through sexual and physical abuse,
it's hard to learn to love yourself. I just couldn't see the
beauty in myself. I masked it well and had most people
fooled. This is why I fell in love with this white powder.
It made me feel invincible, confident, and powerful, not
to mention that it made me skinny. Up until then I had
partied with Jack Daniels and marijuana. This feeling was
so new to me. It quickly showed its true colors. Cocaine

was draining me of money, but more importantly it was stealing my very life from me.

One evening it finally happened. I was home alone, and I collapsed. My heart was beating so fast and loud that it actually sounded like my heart was in my ears. I no longer felt confident and powerful. On the contrary, I felt the exact opposite. I felt beaten, battered and broken. I had managed to inflict these feelings upon myself after managing to get away from others who had inflicted them upon me. This was the first time I felt I wanted to die. This scared me because no matter what had happened to me in the past, I always had a will to live, a drive to prove to everyone that I didn't need them, that I could and would succeed. This was my wake-up call. Something that could make me fly so high could also break me. I parted ways with my love affair with this substance.

My fiancé graduated school and secured a job. He then wanted us to move in with his mother so he could afford to buy a Camaro. Once again, I wasn't good enough to stay with. I will say I'm sure I wasn't the easiest person to have a relationship with. I was still reeling from everything I had been through. I managed to shake my addiction to cocaine, and my partying was pretty much over. I was trying to live a settled-down life with my fiancé. We were just nineteen years old, with so much still to learn. I didn't agree to go because I was proud of my home and what I had achieved. The last thing I wanted was to live with any parents again. He was off to his mother's home. They even took the one thing his mother had bought us for my apartment: a small wooden pantry. I was devastated. My dreams of becoming married and beginning a new life were shattered. I didn't know at the time that it definitely wasn't meant to be. He met the love of his life shortly after leaving me, and they are still happily married. He was not meant to be my partner. We really weren't a good match.

I dated quite a few guys here and there. I had learned the skill of being elusive to men. It drove them crazy that I couldn't care less whether they were around or not. I thought to myself, *I have been through so much in my life. What can anyone possibly do to me that is worse than what has already happened to me?*

My life went on like this for a couple of years. It felt empty, but at least I wasn't getting abused anymore. I was feeling powerful being unkind to men. It was my way of getting back at them for what they had done to me in the past.

It can be a very powerful feeling to hurt others when you are hurting, but it is a false power. I learned that men fall in love with you if you are not that clingy girl, if you are elusive and unkind, but that is false as well. A healthy relationship would not be a part of deceit or unkindness. I was caught in a pattern of attracting men who were emotionally and/or financially unstable themselves. This is a difficult lesson to learn if you are caught in the cycle of unhealthy relationships. You can't see it clearly until you take the time to be on your own to learn. That is the difficult part. When you are in this cycle it just seems the next same guy with a different name is waiting to be your Prince Charming for a while as soon as the previous guy is gone. Being on my own —and notice that I say *being on my own* and not *being alone* —being on my own does not mean I'm alone all the time. I will share my favorite quote: "What a lovely surprise to discover how unlonely being alone can be."

CHAPTER 8

THE ONE

I was going about my business working at the factory, partying with my friends and going through the motions of dating without really caring about any of the guys I was dating. I brushed away the feelings of emptiness by staying busy. Real busy. I kept myself occupied from the time I woke until my head hit the pillow for slumber at night.

Then it happened. I saw a man at work, and I somehow knew he was the man I was going to marry. His name was Stan. He had just arrived in machine shop, where I worked, from another department. Shortly after that, I found out he was married. I couldn't understand why I'd had such a strong feeling of him being the one.

I sure didn't want the drama that came along with trying to date a married man, so I opted to be his friend. He would fix the machines that broke down in my department. I was always jamming up my machine so I could catch a nap to sleep off the cobwebs in my head from partying the night before. He and I got to know each other very well.

I would think of him constantly, and I dreamed of him at night. I always dreamed of him and only him in color. I didn't reveal my real feelings for him . . . until I saw him talking quite often with another woman. It would infuriate me. Here I was trying to hide my feelings for him, and it seemed to me that he was getting quite chummy with this lady. After months of this, I finally blew up in his face. I told him in no uncertain terms how inappropriate I thought his getting close to this woman was. In my tearful expression, I blurted out that I had feelings for him, and how dare he talk to her instead of me? After I was done with my rant, I looked into his eye, and he just had a blank stare going on at me. The humiliation started to grow and grow until it took over my whole body and I just wanted to disappear. I ran off to the bathroom, composed myself, and went back to my machine. What had I just done? This wasn't what I had learned from Jay. It wasn't the sure way of acting aloof with men that made them want me more. I had blown it.

I decided I was going to act like nothing had happened. What else could I do? For the next couple of months, I did just that, and he played along with me. I was so grateful for that. I went back to being his friend without showing him my true feelings.

A couple of months went by, and it was October. My twenty-third birthday had arrived. While I was at work, someone came in to deliver the most beautiful bouquet of white roses to me that I had ever seen. The card had a note attached, but it was signed *Anonymous*. I walked over to the table where we all would take our breaks and proudly showed off my roses. I looked at Stan and said, "I wonder who sent these?" I then rattled off some names of guys I was dating. He didn't say much except that they were nice flowers.

He came up to me later with a birthday card. My heart skipped a beat. I couldn't believe he had remembered my birthday, although I'm sure I hinted to him about it. I opened the card, and I couldn't believe my eyes. I realized the handwriting on the birthday card was the same as the one on the card attached to my roses. I thanked him but didn't say another word until our next break period. I asked him if he was the one who sent me the roses. He asked if we could go to lunch so we could talk. I of course agreed but knew I wouldn't be able to eat. I was so nervous I felt as if a whole kaleidoscope of butterflies were in my stomach. No one had ever made me nervous before. He was someone I respected. Most of the other men in machine shop were always trying to date me or spending their breaks with their noses in a girly magazine. Stan was always respectable, and everyone looked up to him, including me.

Lunch time finally arrived for our department. Stan and I walked to my car. We got in but never left the parking lot. He confessed that he was the one who sent the roses. He said he had feelings for me as well. He didn't tell me the day I yelled at him because, one, he was shocked, and two, he was still married. He went on to explain that he owned a two-flat, and for the past five years his wife had been living on one floor and he on the other. Their marriage was long over except for the paper that declared it. But there had been no reason for a divorce before. He worked and paid the bills. He loved her son as his own and continued to take care of them. The lady he was so chummy with at work was a friend of his wife. They used to work at the same factory years ago. He was talking with her about his plans to finally put the divorce in motion.

He said he respected me too much to ever approach me before he had started the divorce proceedings. I fell so hard in love that very moment. Someone respected me? I had never heard those words or felt what it felt like to even feel respected. All I knew is that it felt damn good!

Even though I was a long way away from being "okay," this was the beginning of me being able to trust and be vulnerable. This is a very valuable lesson. Being vulnerable allows one to not only give love but receive it. Without vulnerability, there are always walls built to block the reception of love. That's a very lonely place to be. It's only fear that makes us avoid being vulnerable. Once you learn to harness your beliefs and learn self-love, you will no longer be afraid. The truth of the matter is that you can open yourself up to anyone. No one truly has the power to take anything from you once you've learned your worth.

CHAPTER 9

My Breakdown

After that lunch break in my car, Stan and I never spent a day apart. We were inseparable. I never knew love could be so wonderful. He stayed with me at my apartment, but he said it was only until he sold the house they had, split the money, and the divorce was final. Then we could get married and have our own home. The thought of having my very own family and being with a man I loved and respected —and, even better, he respected me —was so amazing. I even now am at a loss for words of how to describe it.

I felt safe for the first time in my life. I had hope for a life filled with promise. We secured a new apartment together. I was so excited to start my new life. We had endless talks about how much we loved each other and couldn't wait to be married. We were just waiting for the divorce to be final. His wife was not going to make it easy even though their marriage had been over for years.

Then it happened. I woke up one morning paralyzed with a heart- gripping fear. I was in complete despair. I told Stan I couldn't go to work that day. Little did I know I would never be going back to work there. I couldn't leave my bed. I felt as though I was going insane. Literally insane. Stan called my best friend at the time. She had known me since

I was nine years old and knew all the things I had been through. He explained to her that I was going through some kind of nervous breakdown, and he would like her to come talk with me.

I wouldn't even get out of bed when she visited. She came and sat by my bedside and listened to me. No one including myself could understand what was going on. Here I was soon to marry a wonderful man I loved. Only days ago, I had felt so safe and secure. What was going on? I agreed to see a therapist for the first time in my life.

I never believed in rehashing the past. The night before I was to go to my appointment to see the therapist, I thought long and hard about what was going on. When I arrived at her office and she invited me in to sit down, I already had a script in my head to tell her. She asked me why I was there. I explained I had been absolutely terrified. I was holding on for dear life to any sanity I might have. I told her I believed the thing I feared most was becoming my mother, and here I was becoming a wife soon, which meant I would possibly be becoming a mother soon after that.

She looked at me and said she was shocked that I had such clarity about the reason for feeling the way I did. She said I was halfway through processing what needed to be processed. That was enough for me to believe I could maybe do it on my own. I didn't trust most people, and I wasn't about to put my sanity in the hands of a stranger, no matter what credentials she may have had. I went home and had more and more episodes of terrifying breakdowns. I couldn't understand why Stan wanted to stay with me through this. I was mortified that he was even witnessing this side of me —a side of me I had never even seen before. I had several panic attacks every day.

My cousin came to visit me, and I told her what I was experiencing. She said she had been wondering when I was going to finally fall apart, which only further confirmed to me that it was inevitable that I would become my mother. My father came and took me to church so they could lay their hands upon me and heal me. I was up for anything. I felt I would never feel okay again. I couldn't get married while I was having these episodes.

Stan then had an idea to have my youngest niece and nephew come over for the weekend. He knew I loved them and always had to be a good example for them. They would come stay with me even when I had my first apartment, and whenever they did, I was as clean as a whistle and my first priority was them. No partying with them present. I have three nieces and one nephew.

So here they were. I had to somehow hold it together after several months of dealing with panic attacks and the fear of leaving our apartment. Stan purchased baseball game tickets for us. My niece and nephew were so excited. He somehow knew I would find a way to pull it together for them if no one else. He was right. I managed to get dressed and leave the house with them. Stan then handed me the keys and told me I was driving. I panicked again, but he said he wasn't feeling that well and couldn't drive. I looked at the kids' eager faces and got into the driver's seat, and we arrived in one piece. On the way there, I pleaded with

God in my head. It was a sunny day, but I asked him to show me a rainbow to confirm that I was indeed okay and not going to go insane. We found our seats and got comfortable, and it started to drizzle out of nowhere. Then the biggest rainbow I've ever seen stretched across the sky from one end of the stadium to the other. The announcers excitedly reported it on the broadcast system, and the camera guys made sure the people viewing from home could see it as well. So, there was my answer. All of a sudden, all the months of panic and despair were minimized tremendously. I was going to be okay.

I decided to buy another self-help book, as I was always educating myself on the art of improving myself through learning how to control my mind. I worked daily on improving my state of mind. I had a workbook that prompted me to write out my fears and challenged me to learn more about myself and my thought patterns. I was learning so much and becoming stronger than ever. Panic attacks and the fear that comes along with them are extremely hard. I worked through them without medication. I wanted to fix the underlying problem rather than take a pill to mask it. I had learned from the past that alcohol and drugs, even prescribed drugs, were no longer for me. I also learned that my feeling safe for the first time in my life gave me permission to break down and take the time necessary to do the work to heal properly. For the most part I did. I thought I was out of the woods, and for the most part I was. I still had a lot to work through, and I continued to do so, but I still had a lot of mistakes to make to learn from.

The breakdown was absolutely terrifying. In no way would I ever have believed it was a blessing in disguise. Had it not happened, I would still be suppressing my pain. I would never have taken the time to just stop —just put everything, and I mean everything, on hold. I was forced to take care of myself.

I want to teach people to take care of themselves first, before the breakdown happens. It's a terrifying road to experience, and I wouldn't wish it upon anyone if it can be avoided. It is not a necessary thing to experience in order to heal, but it will happen if you let the pain be suppressed too long. In my case, it was necessary. I gained knowledge of how to handle things like my pain. Doing the work I do now, I am grateful to be able to fully empathize with my clients in a way that someone who has never experienced such things cannot.

CHAPTER 10

BECOMING A MOMMY

We had set the date for our marriage with reassurance that Stan's divorce would certainly end before September. We chose Labor Day weekend, September 5th, 1993. I explained to him that I didn't want to get married if we would end up like the majority of other couples who grew so comfortable that they stopped showing love to each other. I didn't want all the sweet things that we experienced on a daily basis to ever stop. I also knew I needed to feel loved and reassured maybe a bit more than the average person due to my abandonment issues and abuse, especially from men. He promised me it would never happen, and I believed him. After all, we even wrote about our love and memories in a notebook. I wish I still owned that notebook.

Shortly after I was feeling safe and no longer having panic attacks, I began to plan a wedding. I was back to being excited and happy. I was feeling fatigued quite a bit but chalked that up to the stress we were going through with Stan's soon-to-be-ex-wife making things way more difficult than they had to be. He was offering her everything she wanted and more, but she kept asking for even more. I had missed a menstrual cycle. I didn't think much of it because we were using protection. I figured I would buy a test just to set my mind at ease. It was positive. I was pregnant, with three months to go before our wedding date.

I went in the room where Stan was. I don't know why, but I was afraid to tell him. I don't know what I thought would happen. He was always supportive and a rock to lean on for me.

He noticed something different in my look and stance. He asked, " What is it?"

I slowly answered, "I'm pregnant."

He said, " Come here, Mommy," and gave me a big hug.

I think those may have been the sweetest words I ever heard. I was going to be a wife and a mother. Before the fear came creeping back into my mind I quickly and repeatedly kept doing what I needed to do to keep it at bay and control my thoughts. Here I was planning a wedding and the arrival of our child. Life was at its best.

Stan's divorce didn't become final until a week before our wedding date. We had already been together over a year. We were afraid we would have to postpone the wedding, but we marched on with a promise from his lawyer that the divorce would be finalized in time. I had the most beautiful dress. It was a replica of a dress that was used in a wedding for the soap opera *Days of Our Lives*. My father was present, and he accompanied me in the limo to the big, beautiful church where Stan and I were to pledge our lives together.

Most of Stan's family aside from one sister-in-law had become my family. One of my sisters-in-law, Mary, became one of my best friends and remains so to this day. She was my matron of honor. My new family, including my mother-in-law, had assured me that I was not the one who broke up Stan's marriage. Their marriage was in fact over, so I could enjoy my big day without any guilt. What an amazing day. I danced the daddy-daughter dance with my father. I could tell he was so nervous. He was never nervous, so it meant he wanted to dance perfectly for our special dance. Being deaf I'm sure challenged him for the part. He sure didn't miss a beat dancing the rest of the night, though.

Everything was perfect. I didn't mind not drinking, because my child was present inside my belly at our wedding. I even gave up smoking after having smoked two to three packs a day. I never picked the habit up again.

I was so happy. I had a new family, husband, and baby on the way. I never dreamed all this was possible.

The day arrived when I was finally going to meet my baby, Ryan. The labor lasted only two hours from the first contraction to the last. My son came into the world so fast that they couldn't give me any pain medicine at all. I remembered no pain when I looked into his eyes. This time I was able to keep my son. When I laid my eyes on him, my heart opened up with a fierce love I had never known before. I loved Stan very much, and until this very moment I never knew a love deeper even existed. I vowed to protect my son from any harm. I knew with every fiber of my being that absolutely nothing would come between me and my son. I remember feeling sad that my mother didn't feel that feeling towards me —or my father, for that matter. I decided that didn't matter. I was going to be the best mother I could possibly be. Scratch that—even better than the world would even allow me to be. I wasn't going to mess up the now best thing that ever happened to me.

My two favorite men and I got to go home and start our life as a family of three. We couldn't have been happier. Stan left me notes daily before he went to work, and we chatted on the phone on his breaks at work. Back then you had to use a pay phone, so he always made sure he had change on him. I knew I had married the best man on earth, and now I had a little man of his seed to adore as well.

A year later, we purchased our first home. I can't tell you the excitement I felt. I felt as though my heart was going to explode out of my chest. I had gone from a life of complete abuse and depression to a life of happiness and love. We spent many weekends with Stan's brothers and their families. Stan's sister lived in Texas at the time but came in on holidays, and we always spent time together as one big family. I had it all. We bought an old large Victorian house. Stan and his brothers went to work on remodeling it. Stan did most of the work, of course, because his brothers had their own families and homes to tend to, but they helped as much as they could. We had to pretty much gut the whole house, but the part I was most proud of was the beautiful bedroom for my son.

Becoming a mother to my son and daughter was and is the single most important and life- changing event in my life. It only further baffled my mind as to how someone could have children and then mistreat them and throw them away like trash. My love is still very deep and unconditional for them. Had I not had children, I'm not sure I would have ever experienced this kind of love. Parenting after a life of abuse and trauma does not have to be a difficult thing. I teach parents to erase the fear and hopelessness and feel the love. It is life- transforming.

CHAPTER 11
THE LOSS OF A BEAUTIFUL LOVE STORY

When Stan and I had started discussing getting married, I explained something that I knew to be true about myself. I told him that when we got married we would have to maintain the level of love and romance we were now sharing with one another. I had told him I never could be that married couple who drive in a car or share dinner at a restaurant and don't seem to engage with each other at all. I had been through so much abandonment and neglect, and I couldn't bear it if our marriage became a lifeless, going-through-the-motions kind of union. I definitely had a significant amount of insecurities to overcome. He assured me that it would never happen to us. I believed him. After all, he stuck with me through my breakdown, something most men would have run as fast as they could to get away from.

We had more love for each other than I had ever experienced in my life. As time went on in our new home, we both became settled into our routines, as people always do. For the first couple of years he continued to write me notes for me to find while he was at work. I was also putting notes into his lunch for him to find. I know we were happier than most couples were.

We decided to try to have another baby. I was pregnant within two months. We were elated. I just knew it would be a girl. Throughout my pregnancy we maintained a happy home. We were busy remodeling yet another room in anticipation of the arrival of our second child, Aubrey. I couldn't believe things could continue to get better. Our beautiful, perfect daughter was born on a lovely day in May. I now had a son and a daughter. I vowed to fiercely protect them and to provide them with everything they needed, especially love and confidence that I would always be with them no matter what. To this day, even though they are adults, I continue to live up to that vow. They still light up my heart every time I see them.

Aubrey came into this world quickly. I had always known I would have a daughter and that I was going to name her Aubrey. My manifestation had finally arrived. We were so in love with our children. I was so happy, perhaps too happy. Fears that stemmed from my past had no problem rearing their ugly heads. I was awake most nights imagining the unimaginable. I often would wake Stan and tell him about the awful dreams I would have. They were dreams of him treating me as if he didn't care about me at all —very disturbing dreams for me. I was very insecure, and I believe I drove him crazy with my fears of him meeting someone else and leaving me. I finally had everything I had ever dreamed of, and I was terrified that I would lose it all.

I have learned since that people who fear they will suffer are already suffering what they fear, but unfortunately I hadn't yet learned it back then. Stan began to withdraw from me. My worst fear was coming true. He was no longer the romantic guy I adored. He also took a night shift position at work. Our love life was dwindling away. I kept begging for him to get on a day shift position and be at home with our family. I begged him for at least one night a month as a date night. I was desperately trying to hold on and recreate what we had had in the beginning. I begged for about two years to no avail. I was an at-home mom who loved her children with every fiber of her being, but I needed attention and some kind of adult conversation. He would come home from work and either sleep or work on our house all day. The only time I felt he came alive was when we had his brothers and their families over. I was actually jealous because they made him smile and laugh, and I was rarely seeing that side of him anymore.

I was very hurt, and I had that street kid still hiding inside me always. I began to go out with my friends when he was home to watch the kids. I was getting the kind of attention from men I wasn't getting at home. It was wrong to crave and want that attention outside of my marriage, but I felt so lonely. I felt it was inevitable that the marriage would completely die even if we stayed together. What I had shared with him about not being able to be in a marriage that lacked love and attention was now coming true. I had to leave before I got left. I was not going to be abandoned again.

With so much regret and fear, I stirred up enough courage to tell Stan I wanted a divorce. He seemed stunned for a minute. He shared with me that he loved me and wanted to try. He managed to secure a day shift position, and we sought out marriage counseling. It was useless. I was too angry and felt I had fought so long for this and that it was only being addressed now because I said I wanted a divorce. I didn't feel like it was being done because he loved me and wanted me to feel secure, because if that was the case, he would have done it long ago when I was begging for his love and attention.

To be fair, I'm sure it wasn't easy trying to provide for a family and deal with my insecurities as well. We both had managed to mess up what really was a perfect love. While all this trying was going on, he said to me, "You won't make it without me. You will end up in a shitty apartment in a shitty neighborhood." Well, that did it. Time stood still for a moment. I felt a hurt, anger and determination all at once. I'm sure I decided right there and then it was truly over. I no longer even had fear. I have never needed anyone, and I had a new desire to prove I could make it just fine without him.

Our divorce proceedings went fairly well. We both used the same lawyer. I declined to receive any of his 401(k) savings or his pension. I didn't want alimony. I just asked for what the law required him to give for child support. The lawyer advised me to rethink my decision. She said men often would not help above and beyond this, but I kept my decision. I again had to prove I could take care of myself and my children on my own.

On the day of our divorce hearing I had a knot so tight in my stomach I felt as if it would prevent me from even attending. I mustered up all the energy it took to show up and be present. I couldn't hold back the tears while the judge discussed the details of our ending to a perfect love story. I finally let them all go and cried. The judge even asked us if we were sure we wanted to go our separate ways. I didn't really want to. I really wanted Stan to grab me and show me he loved me and was willing to fight for us, but that didn't happen, and anyway I had some things to take care of to prove my independence.

Months later, as my friend and I were clearing out the basement for the sale of our home, she found a bundle of unused Hallmark cards expressing love and devotion. I read them one by one in astonishment. I felt a sadness wash over me, but also anger. He must have bought them with the intention of giving them to me at some point. He never did. I guess we'll never know if it may have changed the course of our separation if he had. Instead of giving me those cards, he said he read a book about why it doesn't make sense to get a divorce because there will always be problems in relationships, so why end one marriage just to get into another one and have to "work" at it again. Not quite the solution I was wanting to hear. I think giving me those cards would have proved to be a much more successful method.

Shortly after the divorce, Stan and I would sometimes get together in some last-ditch efforts to save our marriage. He was understandably upset with me. Probably he was too upset to let bygones be bygones. He treated me as if I had something to make up to him. I didn't agree. On the contrary. . . I believed the opposite.

Then began a sad few years for me. It hurt me deeply that Stan had been so indifferent to me, and I spent many nights crying. It seemed his pride had taken over any part of his heart that ever loved me. I had lost more than a husband; I had lost a best friend. The nightmares I'd had early on about him treating me as if he didn't care at all for me had come true.

Those first few years after the divorce, I wrote several letters to Stan. I still do not know if he ever read them. I never received a reply. Nowadays we are friends and see each other at family get-togethers. I'm glad we were able to rise above everything we had been through. I really don't regret anything in life, but if there was one thing I look back on and wish were different, it would be the demise of our love. I guess if he were to write a book, it would be a different perspective. I'm lucky to not hold any grudges or anger in my heart towards him. In fact, I love him very much and always want what is best for him. He has found a partner he seems very happy with, and I am grateful for that.

CHAPTER 12

DYSFUNCTION CONTINUES

I went on to continue my unhealthy dating patterns for years. I chose men who could just move in with a duffel bag because they didn't own much more. I needed to feel safe and make sure my children were safe. I was the one who owned the home; I was the one who controlled my home. I would eventually tire of their lack of support and contribution and kick them to the curb, only to get into another relationship that would end the same way. This happened repeatedly.

My children always knew my love for them came first. No one I dated was allowed to discipline them. I told each man I dated that my children already had a mother and father, and if he felt my children needed discipline, he was to address me and only me.

I felt I was protecting my children, and in a way I was. They were always secure and knew they were loved beyond measure. I always made sure they had a home that no one could take away from us. I also made sure they went to a private high school, and we traveled as well.

I could have done better in choosing my partners. If I had chosen someone who actually had his life together and was available emotionally, I would have provided a better example to my children. I just didn't trust that someone like that existed. The one man I had married and trusted, in spite of all that had happened to me— even he let me down.

I married two more times. I knew even while getting married that it wouldn't work. I was worn down and agreed to marry them hoping things would change. I even married men who couldn't bring to the table what I could. Once again, they moved into my home, and I would end up divorcing them shortly after marrying them, realizing they were not someone I wanted to spend the rest of my life with.

My third husband was undergoing counseling for anger management to try to stay in our marriage. The counselor pulled me aside after speaking with both of us and said, " You are in a verbally abusive relationship. He is your mother you are still trying to fix." What an eye-opener. I knew I had to stop the insanity. I was good at parenting. I managed to raise two wonderful, happy adults who make healthy choices for themselves, I was able to start businesses, work, and make money, but I still didn't know my self-worth. I kept dating the same dysfunctional men over and over again.

I had a wonderful family and a great circle of friends. How could I have been lacking so badly in the self -worth department? The funny thing is I didn't even know I was. I knew I had no problem getting a man. Even the ones who had it all together wanted to offer me the world. I knew how to stay detached just enough to attract them and at the same time show interest. It's probably an art Jay taught me. I always picked the guy who had little to offer in many ways, such as financially and emotionally. I was secure in starting businesses and getting jobs I went on interviews for. I was never even nervous on interviews —or dates, for that matter. I was brave and made things happen for my children and myself all the time. I had no idea I was insecure. Deep inside, I was frightened. I didn't want to meet the perfect guy and be shattered again. I was abandoned every single time.

How could that ever change? Well, for one, if I had picked guys who were emotionally available, and if I had known what a healthy relationship consisted of, I would have had a much better chance at obtaining one. I had zero chance with the guys I chose.

Nothing is ever guaranteed in a relationship. I will tell you your odds are better when you choose an emotionally healthy partner. That's why it's important to love yourself first. Get healthy, then choose a partner. There are no guarantees, but the odds of a successful relationship will be much better— and if the relationship does end, you love yourself, so it will be easier to heal.

CHAPTER 13

AT HOME AND AT PEACE WITH MYSELF

Fast-forward a bit. Well, maybe a little more than a bit. I have been single (by choice) for just about eleven years. I have been on a couple of dates here and there, but because I have done the work to love myself, I know that even though some of them were very nice men, they were not who I wanted to spend my life with so I didn't waste further time dating them. I have made some exceptional friends through that process.

I am no longer ever lonely when I am alone. It is a welcome time for me to enjoy time with myself, something I could never do in my past. I am completely secure about who I am and how the aging process is taking place. I believe when the right partner comes along I will be able to identify that person. I no longer need anyone. If I choose to spend time with anyone in any capacity, it is because I like being around them. In my current friendships, we enhance each other's lives. It's no longer a one-way street.

I have become a life coach. I help others who have been through trauma and abuse, but I don't limit myself to that. I have enough experience now to help people in many ways. I help with building confidence, and with parenting. I work with children of deaf adults. And I teach the laws of attraction and manifestation, which are about creating a new mindset to create the life you desire. Even through my bad relationships, I maintained a sense of happiness and was able to create a world where I was a single parent who could afford to take my kids out, buy them things they wanted, put them through good schools, and even travel. I did these things by being able to think outside the box and by learning how to manifest.

Once you do the work on yourself, manifesting is a powerful thing to learn. You cannot unlearn it, and you can teach it to others. It's truly a wonderful life if you choose for it to be.

I now have two wonderful grandchildren who fill my life with so much love and joy, in addition to my own children. They bring so much laughter, joy and dance into my life. I am blessed beyond measure, and I intend to help as many others as possible obtain that joy, happiness and success.

* * *

As you can see if you have made it this far in my book, I have been through hell and battled some demons: abuse, neglect, abandonment, eating disorders and addiction, to name a few. I am now a happy person filled with joy and peace. I am a successful business owner. I am a healer. I am a licensed massage therapist, reiki master and life coach.

I promise you, no matter what you've been through, you can achieve whatever you want to succeed. It takes a little work to train your mind. It's no different than any other training process, like training for a marathon or any other type of training. The beauty of learning these tools is you will never want to go back to the "old " way of thinking. You can pass them along to others as well, like your children. Children are my favorite to teach these tools to because they absorb them so quickly. It becomes a way of life to them before they let the world convince them that it is an ugly place, before they start to think *The cards are stacked against me so why even try.*

I now help people step into their self-worth and healing through books, videos, one-on-one sessions and workshops, so that I can teach these tools to as many people as I can. So, know that you are not alone, you matter, and I am here cheering you on. I hope my story has encouraged and supported you on your journey. If I can be of any support, please feel free to reach out to me. You will find my contact information in the About the Author section at the end of this book.

May you hear the sound of sweet freedom whispered in your ears and life. In the next few pages, please find some suggestions to help you on your journey.

TIPS FOR CREATING THE LIFE, RELATIONSHIPS AND BUSINESS YOU WANT

Learning the laws of attraction is primarily important. If your thoughts control you, if you go through life on autopilot and just do your day-to-day things in a tired or thoughtless manner, or if you focus on the lack of anything, that is what the world will present to you. You can shake your head and say this is nonsense, but I'm here to tell you it is real. What do you have to lose by trying? You can control your thoughts and begin to experience happiness and change your life in so many incredible ways. I'm only one of thousands, probably millions, who have experienced this very thing. It's also been proven time and time again scientifically. Aren't your happiness, peace of mind, and success worth a little time in changing your mind and taking control of your life?

Meditation is another important component to obtaining results in a quicker manner. A lot of people say they can't meditate when really they have never given it an honest try. I love meditation, but to be honest I go through phases of not being consistent with it myself. The more consistent I am, the more value I get out of taking time to be still and meditate.

Build in things that bring you joy on a daily basis. Make sure to do things that you enjoy on a daily basis, even if it's only for an hour. Incorporating happiness into your day is so crucial.

Honor and be willing to feel your emotions. Our emotions, good and bad, are a gift. They are indicators of where we are on the scale of the receptive mode. Receptive mode is the state in which you are receiving and accepting the wonderful things that the universe has to give to you. This receiving cannot be done from a place of despair and doubt.

It is good to have a mentor to help guide you along the way. It is my intention to inspire and guide people to achieve happiness, whether they have been through abuse and trauma or have just been taught that happiness, money or success is not in the cards or that success and happiness only come with hard work. That's just not true. Your thoughts and beliefs have everything to do with it. A belief is just a thought you have thought for so long that you believe it to be true.

I will give a quick and simple example of how thoughts can be changed. Now keep in mind this is just a little change in pattern, but it can be a beginning to bigger and better thoughts.

The city where I was born and and have spent my life is Chicago. For most of my life, Chicago has been a beautiful and clean city. I travel a lot, and whenever I visited other cities, I felt proud that the city of Chicago, as big as it is, managed to be one of the cleanest cities I'd seen. For some reason, in 2019 I noticed that my commute to see my clients in the city was polluted with garbage everywhere along the highways and streets. This really aggravated me, because I love my clean, beautiful city. Driving to see my clients always used to be a pleasant drive, but now every day I drove to work my drive was miserable. For weeks I was angry about all the garbage I was seeing. As I mentioned earlier in this chapter, our emotions are an indicator of where we are in our head space, so I was aware, but only after a few weeks of experiencing this feeling of anger and disappointment.

Then I started to take control of my thoughts. I said, well, this is something I have no control over, and hopefully it's temporary, because I can't be the only one noticing it. So I made my complaint to the city, and from then on, instead of looking at the garbage during my commute, I looked upwards. I looked at the beautiful skyline, the beautiful scenery the sky always has on display, and the different motions the waves make on the lake. Now I am no longer disappointed and have joy and happiness on my drives again. I choose not to notice the garbage; I choose to notice the beauty instead.

You may say, "Oh, you choose to stick your head in the sand?" No, I'm choosing where to focus my energy and attention. If I cannot do something about a situation and it is costing me my peace and happiness (which in turn will eventually cost me my health), I choose to think about my blessings instead. This can work with most things if you really do the work. It's a simple method, but it's not always easy. I promise it will bring great rewards, and it's not a process that is painful to do, either.

Hope to see you on the flip side —the side of joy, peace and wellbeing.

ABOUT THE AUTHOR

Once a victim of years of trauma and abuse, Shirley Buck emerged as a beacon of hope for anyone who has suffered similar experiences. Growing up in a toxic environment, she struggled with depression, anxiety and low self-esteem for most of her life. However, through perseverance and a strong desire to heal, she was able to overcome her past and transform into the person she is today.

After years of studying tools to change her mindset and personal growth, Shirley realized that she had a passion for helping others who were going through similar struggles. She decided to become a mindset instructor, using her own experiences as a guide to help others find their way out of dark places.

Shirley's approach to helping others is unique in that she focuses on helping people heal from their trauma, not just move past it. Through her guidance and support, Shirley helps clients develop the necessary tools to live a fulfilling life, free from the weight of their past.

The book serves as a source of inspiration and guidance for anyone who is struggling to find their way out of a difficult situation.

Today, Shirley is a successful mindset instructor, public speaker and advocate for mental health as well as a reiki healer and a public speaker. She is committed to helping others overcome their trauma and live a life of joy and purpose.

You can learn more at her website, Shirleybuck.com.
She also has a private Facebook group called Red Leaf Healing at facebook.com/groups/5905506472827457.
You can reach out to Shirley by email at Healingcoach@ shirleybuck.com.

REVIEWS

"*Sweet Freedom Whispered in My Ear* feels like a beacon of light shining through the darkness. Honest, vulnerable and humble. Kindness and forgiveness flows from the pages, and my heart ached from the pain and anger that must have existed. I love stories of resilience and strength, and this one will stay with me as I look for rainbows in the sky."
—*Tiffani Freckleton, RN, nurse coach, author of* My NICU Story: Written With Love *and co-author of the award-winning international bestseller* Letters to a Future Nurse

"Having shared a bond of friendship with Shirley since our childhood, I found myself deeply familiar with the events narrated in this book. Despite the familiarity, each page was a moving journey, reflecting the courage it must have taken Shirley to publicly share such intimate aspects of her life. Shirley's journey from a turbulent beginning to a place of peace, success and contentment is a testament to this truth. Her strength and compassion shine through every word, making her not only the remarkable teller of her own story but also an inspiration for readers worldwide."
—*Suzanne Mealer*

"The author's deep understanding of trauma and abuse recovery shines through every page, offering practical guidance and real-life situations that readers can relate to. The book combines real-life expertise with a compassionate and humanizing approach, which is both comforting and empowering. It offers a road map to healing that is both informative and deeply inspiring."

—*Courtney Fassett*

"This book has captivated my soul. I've cried, got angry, laughed and more. I wanted to dive into the pages and give young Shirley a hug, but I am absolutely SO proud of the woman she has become. This story is a ministry."

—*Marie Jones, LMT*

"*Sweet Freedom Whispered in My Ear* is a riveting true story of the power of the human spirit's ability to overcome even the most unfathomable traumas. Thank you to first-time author Shirley Buck for baring her soul and so bravely taking us on her emotional journey through self-actualization, showing us that there is hope at the end of the storm. Bravo!"

—*Lisa Molidor, RN*